Strategic Level

Paper P3

Risk Management

EXAM PRACTICE KIT

CIMA

PUBLISHING

KAPLAN

PUBLISHING

Published by: Kaplan Publishing UK

Unit 2 The Business Centre, Molly Millars Lane, Wokingham, Berkshire RG41 2QZ

British Library Cataloguing in Publication Data

A catalogue record for this book is available from the British Library

ISBN: 978-1-78415-146-1

Printed and bound in Great Britain

CONTENTS

	Page
Index to questions and answers	iv
Examination Techniques	v
Syllabus Guidance, Learning Objectives and Verbs	viii
Approach to revision	xi
Present value table	xxi

Section

Quality and accuracy are of the utmost importance to us so if you spot an error in any of our products, please send an email to mykaplanreporting@kaplan.com with full details.

Our Quality Co-ordinator will work with our technical team to verify the error and take action to ensure it is corrected in future editions.

INDEX TO QUESTIONS AND ANSWERS

OBJECTIVE TEST QUESTIONS

EXAM TECHNIQUES

COMPUTER-BASED ASSESSMENT

TEN GOLDEN RULES

1   Make sure you have completed the compulsory 15 minute tutorial before you start exam. This tutorial is available through the CIMA website. You cannot speak to the invigilator once you have started.

2   These exam practice kits give you plenty of exam style questions to practise so make sure you use them to fully prepare.

3   Attempt all questions, there is no negative marking.

4   Double check your answer before you put in the final answer although you can change your response as many times as you like.

5   On multiple choice questions (MCQs), there is only one correct answer.

6   Not all questions will be MCQs – you may have to fill in missing words or figures.

7   Identify the easy questions first and get some points on the board to build up your confidence.

8   Try and allow 15 minutes at the end to check your answers and make any corrections.

9   If you don't know the answer, flag the question and attempt it later. In your final review before the end of the exam try a process of elimination.

10 Work out your answer on the whiteboard provided first if it is easier for you. There is also an onscreen 'scratch pad' on which you can make notes. You are not allowed to take pens, pencils, rulers, pencil cases, phones, paper or notes.

SYLLABUS GUIDANCE, LEARNING OBJECTIVES AND VERBS

A AIMS OF THE SYLLABUS

The aims of the syllabus are

- to provide for the Institute, together with the practical experience requirements, an adequate basis for assuring society that those admitted to membership are competent to act as management accountants for entities, whether in manufacturing, commercial or service organisations, in the public or private sectors of the economy;
- to enable the Institute to examine whether prospective members have an adequate knowledge, understanding and mastery of the stated body of knowledge and skills;
- to complement the Institute's practical experience and skills development requirements.

B STUDY WEIGHTINGS

A percentage weighting is shown against each topic in the syllabus. This is intended as a guide to the proportion of study time each topic requires.

All component learning outcomes will be tested and one question may cover more than one component learning outcome.

The weightings do not specify the number of marks that will be allocated to topics in the examination.

C LEARNING OUTCOMES

Each topic within the syllabus contains a list of learning outcomes, which should be read in conjunction with the knowledge content for the syllabus. A learning outcome has two main purposes:

1   to define the skill or ability that a well-prepared candidate should be able to exhibit in the examination;

2   to demonstrate the approach likely to be taken by examiners in examination questions.

The learning outcomes are part of a hierarchy of learning objectives. The verbs used at the beginning of each learning outcome relate to a specific learning objective, e.g. Evaluate alternative approaches to budgeting.

The verb 'evaluate' indicates a high-level learning objective. As learning objectives are hierarchical, it is expected that at this level students will have knowledge of different budgeting systems and methodologies and be able to apply them.

A list of the learning objectives and the verbs that appear in the syllabus learning outcomes and examinations follows and these will help you to understand the depth and breadth required for a topic and the skill level the topic relates to.

Learning objectives	Verbs used	Definition
1 Knowledge		
What you are expected to know	List	Make a list of
	State	Express, fully or clearly, the details of/ facts of
	Define	Give the exact meaning of
2 Comprehension		
What you are expected to understand	Describe	Communicate the key features of
	Distinguish	Highlight the differences between
	Explain	Make clear or intelligible/State the meaning of
	Identify	Recognise, establish or select after consideration
	Illustrate	Use an example to describe or explain something
3 Application		
How you are expected to apply your knowledge	Apply	To put to practical use
	Calculate/compute	To ascertain or reckon mathematically
	Demonstrate	To prove with certainty or to exhibit by practical means
	Prepare	To make or get ready for use
	Reconcile	To make or prove consistent/ compatible
	Solve	Find an answer to
	Tabulate	Arrange in a table
4 Analysis		
How you are expected to analyse the detail of what you have learned	Analyse	Examine in detail the structure of
	Categorise	Place into a defined class or division
	Compare and contrast	Show the similarities and/or differences between
	Construct	To build up or compile
	Discuss	To examine in detail by argument
	Interpret	To translate into intelligible or familiar terms
	Produce	To create or bring into existence
5 Evaluation		
How you are expected to use your learning to evaluate, make decisions or recommendations	Advise	To counsel, inform or notify
	Evaluate	To appraise or assess the value of
	Recommend	To advise on a course of action
	Advise	To counsel, inform or notify

D OBJECTIVE TEST

The most common types of Objective Test questions are:

- multiple choice, where you have to choose the correct answer from a list of four possible answers. This could either be numbers or text.

- multiple choice with more choices and answers – for example, choosing two correct answers from a list of eight possible answers. This could either be numbers or text.

- single numeric entry, where you give your numeric answer e.g. profit is $10,000.

- multiple entry, where you give several numeric answers e.g. the charge for electricity is $2000 and the accrual is $200.

- true/false questions, where you state whether a statement is true or false e.g. external auditors report to the directors is FALSE.

- matching pairs of text e.g. the convention 'prudence' would be matched with the statement' inventories revalued at the lower of cost and net realisable value'.

- other types could be matching text with graphs and labelling graphs/diagrams.

In this Exam Practice Kit we have used these types of questions.

Some further guidance from CIMA on number entry questions is as follows:

- For number entry questions, you do not need to include currency symbols or other characters or symbols such as the percentage sign, as these will have been completed for you. You may use the decimal point but must not use any other characters when entering an answer (except numbers) so, for example, $10,500.80 would be input as 10500.80

- When expressing a decimal, for example a probability or correlation coefficient, you should include the leading zero (i.e. you should input 0.5 not .5)

- Negative numbers should be input using the minus sign, for example −1000

- You will receive an error message if you try to enter a character or symbol that is not permitted (for example a '£' or '%' sign)

- A small range of answers will normally be accepted, taking into account sensible rounding

Guidance re CIMA On-Screen calculator:

As part of the computer based assessment software, candidates are now provided with a calculator, although they can also use a physical calculator. This calculator is on-screen and is available for the duration of the assessment. The calculator is accessed by clicking the calculator button in the top left hand corner of the screen at any time during the assessment.

All candidates must complete a 15 minute tutorial before the assessment begins and will have the opportunity to familiarise themselves with the calculator and practise using it.

Candidates may practise using the calculator by downloading and installing the practice exam at http://www.vue.com/athena/. The calculator can be accessed from the fourth sample question (of 12).

Please note that the practice exam and tutorial provided by Pearson VUE at http://www.vue.com/athena/ is not specific to CIMA and includes the full range of question types the Pearson VUE software supports, some of which CIMA does not currently use.

The Objective Tests are ninety minute computer-based assessments comprising 60 compulsory questions, with one or more parts. CIMA is continuously developing the question styles within the system and you are advised to try the online website demo at www.cimaglobal.com, to both gain familiarity with assessment software and examine the latest style of questions being used.

APPROACH TO REVISION

Stage 1: Assess areas of strengths and weaknesses

Stage 2: Question practice

Follow the order of revision of topics as recommended in the revision table plan below and attempt the questions in the order suggested.

Try to avoid referring to text books and notes and the model answer until you have completed your attempt.

Try to answer the question in the allotted time.

Review your attempt with the model answer and assess how much of the answer you achieved in the allocated exam time.

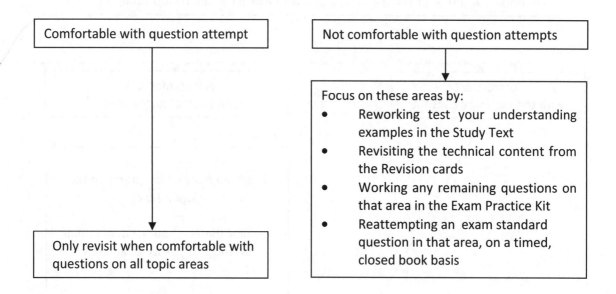

Comfortable with question attempt

Not comfortable with question attempts

Focus on these areas by:
- Reworking test your understanding examples in the Study Text
- Revisiting the technical content from the Revision cards
- Working any remaining questions on that area in the Exam Practice Kit
- Reattempting an exam standard question in that area, on a timed, closed book basis

Only revisit when comfortable with questions on all topic areas

Stage 3: Final pre-exam revision

We recommend that you **attempt at least one ninety minute mock examination** containing a set of previously unseen exam standard questions.

It is important that you get a feel for the breadth of coverage of a real exam without advanced knowledge of the topic areas covered – just as you will expect to see on the real exam day.

Ideally a mock examination offered by your tuition provider should be sat in timed, closed book, real exam conditions.

P3
RISK MANAGEMENT

Syllabus overview

P3 shows how to identify, evaluate and manage various risks that could adversely affect the implementation of the organisation's strategy. It provides the competencies required to analyse, evaluate and apply the techniques, processes and internal control systems required to manage risk. This insight is then used to manage the risks associated with both cash flows and capital investment decisions – two important areas of organisational life for which the finance function is responsible.

Summary of syllabus

Weight	Syllabus topic
20%	A. Identification, classification and evaluation of risk
20%	B. Responses to strategic risk
20%	C. Internal controls to manage risk
20%	D. Managing risks associated with cash flows
20%	E. Managing risks associated with capital investment decisions

P3 – A. IDENTIFICATION, CLASSIFICATION AND EVALUATION OF RISK (20%)

Learning outcomes
On completion of their studies, students should be able to:

Lead	Component		Indicative syllabus content
1 evaluate the types of risk facing an organisation and recommend appropriate responses.	(a)	identify the types of risk facing an organisation	• Upside and downside risks arising from internal and external sources and from different managerial decisions. • Risks arising from international operations, such as cultural differences and differences between legal systems. **Note:** No specific real country will be tested. • Strategic and operational risks.
	(b)	evaluate the organisation's ability to bear identified risks	• Quantification of risk exposures (impact if an adverse event occurs) and their expected values, taking account of likelihood. • Risk map representation of risk exposures as a basis for reporting and analysing risks.
	(c)	recommend responses to identified risks.	• Enterprise Risk Management and its components. • Risk mitigation including TARA – transfer, avoid, reduce, accept. • Gross and net risks. • Assurance mapping and similar techniques for describing risks and their associated responses.
2 evaluate senior management's responsibility for the implementation of risk management strategies and internal controls.	(a)	recommend techniques that will enable the board to discharge its responsibilities with respect to managing risks	• The control environment. • Internal control. • Risk register.
	(b)	advise the board on its responsibilities for reporting risks to shareholders and other stakeholders.	• Risk reports and stakeholder responses.
3 evaluate the ethical impact of risk.	(a)	evaluate ethical, social and environmental issues arising from risk management.	• The identification of ethical dilemmas associated with risk management. • Reputational risks associated with social and environmental impacts.

P3 – B. RESPONSES TO STRATEGIC RISK (20%)

Learning outcomes
On completion of their studies, students should be able to:

Lead	Component	Indicative syllabus content
1 evaluate the tools and processes required for strategy implementation.	(a) recommend appropriate measures for the strategic control and direction of various types of organisations	<ul><li>Business unit performance and appraisal, including transfer pricing and taxation, reward systems and incentives.</li><li>Non-financial measures and their interaction with financial measures.</li><li>Risks of performance measurement, including the Balanced Scorecard (BSC).</li><li>Lean systems.</li><li>Cost of quality.</li><li>Big Data as a strategic resource.</li></ul>
	(b) recommend solutions for the risks of dysfunctional behaviour arising from the associated models of performance measurement	<ul><li>Dysfunctional behaviour associated with measures of control and direction.</li></ul>
	(c) advise managers of the risks in the development of strategies for information systems that support the organisation's strategic requirements.	<ul><li>The purpose and contents of information systems strategies, and the need for strategy complementary to the corporate and individual business strategies.</li></ul>
2 evaluate ethical issues facing an organisation and its employees.	(a) evaluate the risks of unethical behaviour.	<ul><li>Ethical issues identified in the CIMA Code of Ethics for Professional Accountants.</li><li>Application of the CIMA Code of Ethics for Professional Accountants.</li><li>The board's responsibilities for the management of stakeholders' interests.</li></ul>
3 evaluate the risks associated with corporate governance.	(a) evaluate the risks associated with poor governance structures.	<ul><li>The separation of the roles of CEO and chairman.</li><li>The role of non-executive directors.</li><li>The roles of audit committee, remuneration committee, risk committee and nominations committee.</li><li>Directors' remuneration.</li><li>The agency implications of salaries, bonuses, performance-related pay, executive share options and benefits in kind.</li></ul>

P3 – C. INTERNAL CONTROLS TO MANAGE RISK (20%)

Learning outcomes
On completion of their studies, students should be able to:

Lead	Component	Indicative syllabus content
1 evaluate control systems for organisational activities and resources.	(a) evaluate the appropriateness of control systems for the management of an organisation.	• Application of control systems and related theory to the design of management accounting control systems and information systems in general. • Control systems within functional areas of a business including HR, sales, purchases, treasury, distribution, IT. • Identification of appropriate responsibility and control centres within the organisation. • Performance target setting. • Performance appraisal and feedback. • Cost of quality applied to the management accounting function and 'getting things right first time'. • Responses to risks in control systems for management.
2 evaluate risk management strategies and internal controls.	(a) evaluate the essential features of internal control systems for identifying, assessing and managing risks.	• Minimising the risk of fraud: fraud policy statements, effective recruitment policies and good internal controls, such as approval procedures and separation of functions. • The risk manager role as distinct from that of internal auditor. • Purposes of internal control: the achievement of an entity's objectives, effectiveness and efficiency of operations. • Identifying and evaluating control weaknesses. • Identifying and evaluating compliance failures. • Operational features of internal control systems, including embedding such systems in a company's operations, responsiveness to evolving risks and timely reporting to management.

Learning outcomes
On completion of their studies, students should be able to:

Lead	Component	Indicative syllabus content
		• The pervasive nature of internal control and the need for employee training. • Costs and benefits of maintaining the internal control system. • Disaster recovery.
3 evaluate the purposes and process of audit in the context of internal control systems.	(a) evaluate the effective planning and management of internal audit and internal audit investigations.	• Forms of internal audit: compliance audit, fraud investigation, value for money audit/management audit, social and environmental audit. • Operation of internal audit, the assessment of audit risk and the process of analytical review, including different types of benchmarking, their use and limitations. • Effective internal audit: independence, staffing and resourcing, organisational remit. • The preparation and interpretation of the internal audit report.

P3 – D. MANAGING RISKS ASSOCIATED WITH CASH FLOW S (20%)

Learning outcomes
On completion of their studies, students should be able to:

Lead	Component	Indicative syllabus content
1 evaluate financial risks facing an organisation.	(a) evaluate financial risks facing an organisation.	• Sources of financial risk associated with international operations. • Transaction, translation, economic and political risk. • Quantification of risk exposures, their sensitivities to changes in external conditions and their expected values. • Exposure to interest rate risks.
2 evaluate alternative risk management tools.	(a) advise on the effects of economic factors that affect future cash flows from international operations	• Exchange rate theory and the impact of differential inflation rates on forecast exchange rates. • Theory and forecasting of exchange rates (e.g. interest rate parity, purchasing power parity and the Fisher effect). • Value at risk.
	(b) evaluate appropriate methods for the identification and management of financial risks associated with international operations	• Minimising political risk. • Responses to economic transaction and translation risks. • Operation and features of the more common instruments for managing interest rate risk: swaps, forward rate agreements, futures and options. • Techniques for combining options in order to achieve a specific risk profile: caps, collars and floors. • Internal hedging techniques.
	(c) evaluate appropriate methods for the identification and management of financial risks associated with debt finance.	• Operation and features of the more common instruments for managing currency risk: swaps, forward contracts, money market hedges, futures and options. **Note :** The Black Scholes option pricing model will not be tested numerically. However, an understanding of the variables which will influence the value of an option will be assumed.

P3 – E. MANAGING RISKS ASSOCIATED WITH CAPITAL INVESTMENT DECISIONS (20%)

Learning outcomes
On completion of their studies, students should be able to:

Lead	Component	Indicative syllabus content
1 evaluate the risks arising from changes in the environment for capital investment appraisal.	(a) evaluate investment projects	<ul><li>Cost of capital and risk.</li><li>Recognising risk using the certainty equivalent method (when given a risk free rate and certainty equivalent values).</li><li>Adjusted present value. **Note:** The two step method may be tested for debt introduced permanently and debt in place for the duration of the project.</li></ul>
	(b) evaluate conflicts that may arise from capital investment decisions	<ul><li>Managing conflicts between different stakeholder groups (profit maximisation versus wealth maximisation).</li><li>Managing conflicts arising from performance indicators.</li></ul>
	(c) evaluate the outcomes of projects post implementation and post completion.	<ul><li>Monitoring the implementation of plans.</li><li>Post completion audit.</li></ul>

PRESENT VALUE TABLE

Present value of 1.00 unit of currency, that is $(1+r)^{-n}$ where r = interest rate; n = number of periods until payment or receipt.

Periods	Interest rates (r)									
(n)	1%	2%	3%	4%	5%	6%	7%	8%	9%	10%
1	0.990	0.980	0.971	0.962	0.952	0.943	0.935	0.926	0.917	0.909
2	0.980	0.961	0.943	0.925	0.907	0.890	0.873	0.857	0.842	0.826
3	0.971	0.942	0.915	0.889	0.864	0.840	0.816	0.794	0.772	0.751
4	0.961	0.924	0.888	0.855	0.823	0.792	0.763	0.735	0.708	0.683
5	0.951	0.906	0.863	0.822	0.784	0.747	0.713	0.681	0.650	0.621
6	0.942	0.888	0.837	0.790	0.746	0.705	0.666	0.630	0.596	0.564
7	0.933	0.871	0.813	0.760	0.711	0.665	0.623	0.583	0.547	0.513
8	0.923	0.853	0.789	0.731	0.677	0.627	0.582	0.540	0.502	0.467
9	0.914	0.837	0.766	0.703	0.645	0.592	0.544	0.500	0.460	0.424
10	0.905	0.820	0.744	0.676	0.614	0.558	0.508	0.463	0.422	0.386
11	0.896	0.804	0.722	0.650	0.585	0.527	0.475	0.429	0.388	0.350
12	0.887	0.788	0.701	0.625	0.557	0.497	0.444	0.397	0.356	0.319
13	0.879	0.773	0.681	0.601	0.530	0.469	0.415	0.368	0.326	0.290
14	0.870	0.758	0.661	0.577	0.505	0.442	0.388	0.340	0.299	0.263
15	0.861	0.743	0.642	0.555	0.481	0.417	0.362	0.315	0.275	0.239
16	0.853	0.728	0.623	0.534	0.458	0.394	0.339	0.292	0.252	0.218
17	0.844	0.714	0.605	0.513	0.436	0.371	0.317	0.270	0.231	0.198
18	0.836	0.700	0.587	0.494	0.416	0.350	0.296	0.250	0.212	0.180
19	0.828	0.686	0.570	0.475	0.396	0.331	0.277	0.232	0.194	0.164
20	0.820	0.673	0.554	0.456	0.377	0.312	0.258	0.215	0.178	0.149

Periods	Interest rates (r)									
(n)	11%	12%	13%	14%	15%	16%	17%	18%	19%	20%
1	0.901	0.893	0.885	0.877	0.870	0.862	0.855	0.847	0.840	0.833
2	0.812	0.797	0.783	0.769	0.756	0.743	0.731	0.718	0.706	0.694
3	0.731	0.712	0.693	0.675	0.658	0.641	0.624	0.609	0.593	0.579
4	0.659	0.636	0.613	0.592	0.572	0.552	0.534	0.516	0.499	0.482
5	0.593	0.567	0.543	0.519	0.497	0.476	0.456	0.437	0.419	0.402
6	0.535	0.507	0.480	0.456	0.432	0.410	0.390	0.370	0.352	0.335
7	0.482	0.452	0.425	0.400	0.376	0.354	0.333	0.314	0.296	0.279
8	0.434	0.404	0.376	0.351	0.327	0.305	0.285	0.266	0.249	0.233
9	0.391	0.361	0.333	0.308	0.284	0.263	0.243	0.225	0.209	0.194
10	0.352	0.322	0.295	0.270	0.247	0.227	0.208	0.191	0.176	0.162
11	0.317	0.287	0.261	0.237	0.215	0.195	0.178	0.162	0.148	0.135
12	0.286	0.257	0.231	0.208	0.187	0.168	0.152	0.137	0.124	0.112
13	0.258	0.229	0.204	0.182	0.163	0.145	0.130	0.116	0.104	0.093
14	0.232	0.205	0.181	0.160	0.141	0.125	0.111	0.099	0.088	0.078
15	0.209	0.183	0.160	0.140	0.123	0.108	0.095	0.084	0.079	0.065
16	0.188	0.163	0.141	0.123	0.107	0.093	0.081	0.071	0.062	0.054
17	0.170	0.146	0.125	0.108	0.093	0.080	0.069	0.060	0.052	0.045
18	0.153	0.130	0.111	0.095	0.081	0.069	0.059	0.051	0.044	0.038
19	0.138	0.116	0.098	0.083	0.070	0.060	0.051	0.043	0.037	0.031
20	0.124	0.104	0.087	0.073	0.061	0.051	0.043	0.037	0.031	0.026

Please check the CIMA website for the latest version of the maths tables and formulae sheets in advance of sitting your live assessment.

Cumulative present value of 1.00 unit of currency per annum, Receivable or Payable at the end of each year for n years $\frac{1-(1+r)^{-n}}{r}$

Periods	Interest rates (r)									
(n)	1%	2%	3%	4%	5%	6%	7%	8%	9%	10%
1	0.990	0.980	0.971	0.962	0.952	0.943	0.935	0.926	0.917	0.909
2	1.970	1.942	1.913	1.886	1.859	1.833	1.808	1.783	1.759	1.736
3	2.941	2.884	2.829	2.775	2.723	2.673	2.624	2.577	2.531	2.487
4	3.902	3.808	3.717	3.630	3.546	3.465	3.387	3.312	3.240	3.170
5	4.853	4.713	4.580	4.452	4.329	4.212	4.100	3.993	3.890	3.791
6	5.795	5.601	5.417	5.242	5.076	4.917	4.767	4.623	4.486	4.355
7	6.728	6.472	6.230	6.002	5.786	5.582	5.389	5.206	5.033	4.868
8	7.652	7.325	7.020	6.733	6.463	6.210	5.971	5.747	5.535	5.335
9	8.566	8.162	7.786	7.435	7.108	6.802	6.515	6.247	5.995	5.759
10	9.471	8.983	8.530	8.111	7.722	7.360	7.024	6.710	6.418	6.145
11	10.368	9.787	9.253	8.760	8.306	7.887	7.499	7.139	6.805	6.495
12	11.255	10.575	9.954	9.385	8.863	8.384	7.943	7.536	7.161	6.814
13	12.134	11.348	10.635	9.986	9.394	8.853	8.358	7.904	7.487	7.103
14	13.004	12.106	11.296	10.563	9.899	9.295	8.745	8.244	7.786	7.367
15	13.865	12.849	11.938	11.118	10.380	9.712	9.108	8.559	8.061	7.606
16	14.718	13.578	12.561	11.652	10.838	10.106	9.447	8.851	8.313	7.824
17	15.562	14.292	13.166	12.166	11.274	10.477	9.763	9.122	8.544	8.022
18	16.398	14.992	13.754	12.659	11.690	10.828	10.059	9.372	8.756	8.201
19	17.226	15.679	14.324	13.134	12.085	11.158	10.336	9.604	8.950	8.365
20	18.046	16.351	14.878	13.590	12.462	11.470	10.594	9.818	9.129	8.514

Periods	Interest rates (r)									
(n)	11%	12%	13%	14%	15%	16%	17%	18%	19%	20%
1	0.901	0.893	0.885	0.877	0.870	0.862	0.855	0.847	0.840	0.833
2	1.713	1.690	1.668	1.647	1.626	1.605	1.585	1.566	1.547	1.528
3	2.444	2.402	2.361	2.322	2.283	2.246	2.210	2.174	2.140	2.106
4	3.102	3.037	2.974	2.914	2.855	2.798	2.743	2.690	2.639	2.589
5	3.696	3.605	3.517	3.433	3.352	3.274	3.199	3.127	3.058	2.991
6	4.231	4.111	3.998	3.889	3.784	3.685	3.589	3.498	3.410	3.326
7	4.712	4.564	4.423	4.288	4.160	4.039	3.922	3.812	3.706	3.605
8	5.146	4.968	4.799	4.639	4.487	4.344	4.207	4.078	3.954	3.837
9	5.537	5.328	5.132	4.946	4.772	4.607	4.451	4.303	4.163	4.031
10	5.889	5.650	5.426	5.216	5.019	4.833	4.659	4.494	4.339	4.192
11	6.207	5.938	5.687	5.453	5.234	5.029	4.836	4.656	4.486	4.327
12	6.492	6.194	5.918	5.660	5.421	5.197	4.988	4.793	4.611	4.439
13	6.750	6.424	6.122	5.842	5.583	5.342	5.118	4.910	4.715	4.533
14	6.982	6.628	6.302	6.002	5.724	5.468	5.229	5.008	4.802	4.611
15	7.191	6.811	6.462	6.142	5.847	5.575	5.324	5.092	4.876	4.675
16	7.379	6.974	6.604	6.265	5.954	5.668	5.405	5.162	4.938	4.730
17	7.549	7.120	6.729	6.373	6.047	5.749	5.475	5.222	4.990	4.775
18	7.702	7.250	6.840	6.467	6.128	5.818	5.534	5.273	5.033	4.812
19	7.839	7.366	6.938	6.550	6.198	5.877	5.584	5.316	5.070	4.843
20	7.963	7.469	7.025	6.623	6.259	5.929	5.628	5.353	5.101	4.870

Section 1

OBJECTIVE TEST QUESTIONS

IDENTIFICATION, CLASSIFICATION AND EVALUATION OF RISK

A1: TYPES OF RISK

1   **Which one of the following sentences best describes risk?**

   A   The exposure to the adverse consequences of dangerous environments

   B   The expected impact of uncertain future events on objectives

   C   The chance of being caught doing something unethical

   D   The impact of the exposure to the adverse consequences of uncertain future events

2   **Risk management is the process of reducing the adverse consequences either by reducing the _____ of an event or its _____.**

   What are the two missing words?

   A   Understanding and impact

   B   Likelihood and potential

   C   Understanding and potential

   D   Likelihood and impact

3   **Risk appetite is determined by**

   A   Risk attitude and risk awareness

   B   Risk attitude and risk capacity

   C   Risk strategy and risk awareness

   D   Risk attitude and residual risk

4   **The four strategies in TARA for managing risk do NOT include which one of the following?**

   A   Transference

   B   Approval

   C   Avoidance

   D   Acceptance

5   Risks can be categorised as either 'pure', 'speculative' or 'upside'. Drag and drop the
    following risks into the correct category.

2

	Pure risks	Speculative risks
The risk that a fire may destroy company assets	✓	
The risk that a customer goes out of business		✓
The risk that a foreign exchange rate may change		✓
The risk relating to the level of future profits		✓
The risk that a capital investment may not yield the predicted IRR		✓
The risk that a virus is introduced to a computer application	✓	

6   There are six steps in CIMA's risk management cycle. Identify the correct sequence of
    steps, by entering step numbers below.

Development of risk response strategy	3
Implement strategy and allocate responsibilities	4
Review and refine process and do it again	6
Identify risk areas	2
Implementation and monitoring of controls	5
Understand and assess scale of risk	1

7   Match each of the following risks to the appropriate risk category.

Risk category		Risk	
Business risks	1	Inflation rate rises	3
Economic risks	3	Exchange rate changes	4
Environmental risks	2	Failure of a new product	1
Financial risks	4	Rate of climate change increases	2

8   Match each of the following risks to the appropriate risk category.

Risk category		Risk	
Business risks	3	CEO convicted of insider dealing	1
Economic risks	2	Disposable income levels fall	2
Corporate reputation risks	1	Nationalisation of industry	4
Political risks	4	Raw material prices rise	3

9   Match each of the following risks to the appropriate risk category.

Risk category		Risk	
Political risks	2	Government increases rate of Corporation Tax	3
Legal risks	1	Company prosecuted for breach of the Data Protection Act	4
Regulatory risks	3	Change of Government	2
Compliance risks	4	Customer sues company for negligence	1

10 X is a food manufacturer. X uses genetically modified (GM) ingredients in some of its products. A change in public opinion regarding GM foods represents which of the following types of risk? (One only)

    A   Business risk

    B   Economic risk

    C   Reputation risk

    D   Environmental risk

11 AA plc is a multinational company, retailing household electrical appliances. The finance director is concerned about the lack of risk management as at the present time AA plc only look at financial risk.

Select THREE of the following risk categories that would also be relevant for AA plc to assess

    A   Gearing

    B   Product risk

    C   Reputation risk

    D   Risk response

    E   Technological risk

    F   Monitoring Risk

12 Viva plc is a large casino company, operating all over the world. Each casino is a multi-million pound construction project. Viva plc's current policy is to finance expansion using high debt levels

Which THREE of the following risks would you identify as critical for Viva to assess?

    A   Financial risk

    B   Project risk

    C   Foreign Exchange rate risk

    D   Production risk

    E   Health and safety risk

    F   commodity price risk

13   OKJ is currently undertaking a risk analysis.

Which TWO of the following factors are the most important risk issues facing OKJ?

A   OKJ's home country has recently elected a new government. It is not yet clear if they will introduce new legislation to increase minimum wages. This would have a major impact on IOS's profitability.

B   After a recent accident in one of its factories, OKJ was convicted of breaching relevant health and safety legislation. Based on similar recent cases brought in the industry, OKJ expects to be fined around 7% of its turnover. OKJ has insurance in place that will cover this fine.

C   OKJ uses platinum as a key component within some of its products. The price of metals varies significantly on world markets and tends to rise sharply in times of recession. The directors are concerned that its products may become unprofitable if platinum prices rise more than 20% from their current levels, but is uncertain about whether this would happen – even if a recession does occur.

D   OKJ is uncertain about whether it can retain its CEO in the long term. It has had a number of CEO's over the last five years – each of them staying very different lengths of time in their roles. Fortunately, OKJ has an experienced Board of Directors and the change in CEOs has had little impact on the business in the past.

14   One of the first steps in developing a risk management strategy is to determine the risk capacity, attitude and appetite of the organisation. Match the definitions with the terms below:

Term	Definition
risk capacity 2	'the overall approach to risk' 1
risk attitude 1	'the amount of risk that the organisation is willing to accept in the pursuit of value added' 3
risk appetite 3	'the amount of risk that the organisation is able to bear' 2

15   The Board of X is discussing risk. The first item for discussion is the organisation's 'risk appetite'. Which of the following factors determine the risk appetite of an organisation? (Select ALL correct answers)

A   The background of the board

B   The number of directors

C   The reputation of X

D   The nature of the product or service of X

E   Customer expectations

16   The identification of risk is an important stage in developing a risk management strategy. Approaches to identifying risk are categorised as internal or external, and proactive or reactive.

The use of SWOT and PEST(EL) analysis are both examples of which approach?

A   internal proactive

B   internal reactive

C   external proactive

D   external reactive

17   'Be A Sport Ltd' is a medium-sized event organiser and is considering the following four possible strategies and how best to manage the risks involved:

    1   A race event Be A Sport Ltd has organised for next week is an outdoors 5k run. However if it rains it is unlikely to attract enough competitors to make any profit. The management have decided to still hold the event.

    2   Be A Sport Ltd has just taken out a large insurance contract to ensure they are covered if any competitor seeks damages for injuries caused in one of their races.

    3   One of the employees at Be A Sport Ltd has had an innovative idea to hold a waterfall jumping event where competitors compete to jump from the highest possible place along a sheer cliff edge into the North Sea. After considering the idea the Be A Sport Ltd management have rejected it as it is too dangerous.

    4   As part of the organisation of the huge annual showcase event Be A Sport Ltd hold, they have conducted a large and extensive risk assessment process and put into place all the internal controls they believe to be necessary.

Which strategy best fits the following four risk management methods?

A   Transfer   2

B   Accept   1

C   Reduce   4

D   Avoid   3

18   X is a company involved in oil exploration and extraction. Following a risk review, X has identified that earthquakes occur in its exploration areas once every five years, on average. The average cost of work to resume oil production, following an earthquake, is estimated to be US$ 30million.

Calculate the value of the risk of earthquakes, in US$, to the nearest million.

19   X is a financial institution, lending to consumers for the purchase of consumer durables. X currently has a total of £120 million lent to customers, and currently has 200,000 loans outstanding to customers. The management accountant of X has calculated that the likelihood of a customer defaulting on a loan is 2%.

What is the 'credit risk exposure' of X, on its consumer lending? Express your answer in £, rounded to the nearest million.

20   D, a finance manager, has been asked to forecast the sales for next year. The standard calculation with the organisation is to account for various probable outcomes using expected values. D has been given the following information by the Sales Manager

Forecast sales for next year	Probability of occurrence
£200,000	10%
£250,000	40%
£300,000	30%
£350,000	20%

Calculate which ONE of the following is the EXPECTED value of Sales for next year?

A   £200,000

B   £260,000

C   £280,000

D   £240,000

21   Party Ltd is a successful family-run business retailing party ware from a small shop in the UK. The younger members of the business wish to open another larger shop in a neighbouring town and to expand into e-business, selling across the country via the Internet. However, the Managing Director, founder and mother of the younger family members has resisted all change and says that the business is doing fine without any change, so there is no reason to do anything.

Which ONE of the following Risk attitudes can you see being displayed by the Managing Director?

A   Risk seeking

B   Risk cautious

C   Risk averse

D   Risk taker

22   'Risk mapping' is a technique that is commonly used to show risks on a matrix. Which TWO variables form the 'axes' or 'dimensions' of a risk map?

A   Source

B   Category

C   Probability

D   Department

E   Impact

23   The sudden death of the CEO of a small marketing consultancy would best fit which category in a risk map?

A   Low probability; low impact

B   Low probability; high impact

C   High probability; low impact

D   High probability; high impact

24   X is a large retailer, employing over 20,000 sales staff. The retail industry has a reputation for a high level of staff turnover. The resignation of a member of the sales staff would best fit which category in a risk map?

A   Low probability; low impact

B   Low probability; high impact

C   High probability; low impact

D   High probability; high impact

25   The 'TARA' mnemonic is often used to categorise risk management methods. Which of the following represents the methods in the TARA mnemonic? (ONE ONLY)

A   Transfer; Assure; Remove; Accept

B   Transfer; Accept; Reduce; Adapt

C   Transfer; Avoid; Reduce; Accept

D   Transfer; Accept; Remove; Adapt

26 'Net risk' (also known as 'residual risk') is calculated by multiplying probability and impact _____ any action is taken to mitigate the risk.

Which word correctly completes the sentence above?

A   Before

B   After

A2: SENIOR MANAGEMENT RESPONSIBILITY FOR RISK MANAGEMENT

27 F, an internal auditor working for ABC plc, a medium-sized building contractor firm, is concerned with the risk management process with ABC. F has investigated the process at each organisational level extensively and found that, although ABC do identify risks and then respond, the cognitive process involved in analysing the likelihood and impact for each identified risk is not being systematically conducted

Distinguish which ONE of the following steps are missing from ABC's risk management process

A   Control activities

B   Reporting

C   Risk Assessment

D   Compliance

28 The Committee of Sponsoring Organisations of the Treadway Commission (2003) have developed a three dimensional matrix Enterprise Risk management (ERM) framework

Which THREE are the missing elements of the ERM framework pictured above.

A   Division

B   Monitoring

C   Internal environment

D   PEST

E   core competencies

F   Analysis

29   The Committee of Sponsoring Organisations (COSO) outlined six key principles of
      Enterprise Risk Management (ERM). Identify which of the following is/are included.
      (Select ALL correct answers)

      A   Consideration of risk management in the context of business strategy

      B   The creation of a risk aware culture

      C   Consideration of a narrow range of risks, mainly financial

      D   Risk management is the responsibility of the Risk Committee

      E   A comprehensive and holistic approach to risk management

30   X is planning to produce its first 'risk register'. Which of the following aspects of each risk
      should be included in such a document? (Select ALL correct answers)

      A   The probability or likelihood of the risk

      B   The name of the risk owner

      C   Actions to be taken to mitigate the risk

      D   The impact of the risk

      E   The level of residual risk associated with the risk

31   In 1992, the Committee of Sponsoring Organisations (COSO) stated that an effective
      internal control system consists of five integrated elements. Which of the following are
      elements of such a system, according to COSO? (Select ALL correct answers)

      A   Risk assessment

      B   A risk register

      C   An internal audit function

      D   A control environment

      E   Control activities

32   Health plc is a leading innovative pharmaceutical research and manufacturing company
      with interests across the globe. Yesterday a leading newspaper in a developing country
      exposed a serious and potentially deadly health risk to employees being exposed to
      harmful chemicals.

      Health plc has not yet reacted to the report in the management are in emergency
      meetings to decide on the best course of action. Within the meeting the newly appointed
      Finance Manager remarked on the lack of regard for employees by local managers and a
      culture of carelessness and neglect.

      Which ONE element of the COSO framework for Internal controls is the Finance Manager
      discussing?

      A   Control environment

      B   Risk assessment

      C   Control activities

      D   Monitoring

33 According to the Financial Reporting Council (FRC) in its version of the Turnbull Report, which of the following is ultimately responsible for a company's system of internal controls?

  A   The Financial Controller

  B   The Board of Directors

  C   The Internal Audit function

  D   Every employee

34 The influential in the UK Turnbull report (1992), stated there are three features of a sound internal control system

Which THREE of the following best describes those three features within the Turnbull report?

  A   The principle of Internal control is embedded into the organisation.

  B   The board of Director must resign if any internal control failure is found.

  C   An organisations' internal control system must be able to respond to changing risks from within and outside the company.

  D   An internal auditor must be appointed by every organisation.

  E   The internal control system must include a robust and rigorous procedure for reporting.

  F   The shareholders must be informed of all internal controls in place in the annual report.

35 X is a retailer of fruit and vegetables. X has recently acquired a number of farm businesses. This is an example of which type of integration?

  A   Forward Vertical

  B   Backward Vertical

  C   Horizontal

  D   Conglomerate

A3: THE ETHICAL IMPACT OF RISK

36 X is concerned about risks to its corporate reputation. Identify which of the following risks directly affect the reputation of X? (Select ALL correct answers)

  A   A key supplier of X is based in a 'low wage economy', and is known by X to employ staff as young as 8 years of age.

  B   The packaging used by X is not recyclable, and contains small traces of a known toxin.

  C   X delivers its products by road and air.

  D   X pays staff at levels below the average for its industry.

  E   X does business with several non-democratic or repressive governments.

37   MLC is a clothing retailer who imports clothes from diverse suppliers worldwide. MLC has a very strong, well publicised corporate ethical code. The company accountant has just found out that one of MLC suppliers use child labour in the manufacture of their clothes and pay very low wages with cramped, dangerous conditions. This is in breach of contract conditions with that supplier.

What actions should MLC take in the light of this?

A   Place more orders with the supplier – it's cheap labour so the margins are good, which should keep the shareholders happy.

B   Leave things as they are and hope the information doesn't get out.

C   Continue trading with the supplier but investigate the claims quietly.

D   Cancel all contracts with the supplier and release a press statement stating how the company will always act quickly and decisively if unethical practices are suspected.

38   The legal position of the whistleblower is covered within the Public Interest Disclosure Act 1998. Under that Act, 'malpractice' can take which of the following forms? (Select ALL correct answers)

A   Criminal offences

B   Failure to comply with a legal obligation

C   Miscarriage of justice

D   Threats to health and safety

E   Damage to the environment

39   You are a management accountant working a UK listed chemical company. During the course of your duties, you become aware that the company is dumping waste illegally. You have raised this with your manager who has told you to ignore the issue.

Which of the following is NOT an appropriate course of action to take next?

A   Contacting CIMA's ethical helpline for advice

B   Reporting the company to the environment agency

C   Contacting a journalist at a national newspaper

D   Taking the matter to the Audit committee

40   Which THREE of the following are common arguments FOR organisations adopting a strong approach to corporate social responsibility (CSR)?

A   Increased profitability due to cost reductions

B   Faster strategic decision-making

C   Improved reputation with environmentally conscious customers

D   Ability to attract higher calibre staff

E   Reduced risk of government intervention in the future

RESPONSES TO STRATEGIC RISK

B1: TOOLS AND PROCESSES FOR STRATEGY IMPLEMENTATION

41 **XYZ is a medium sized pharmaceutical company. XC has at present a decentralised structure with five separate autonomous divisions divided by clinical need, for example. Division A focuses on cancer research, Division B on topical diseases, etc. Expertise is highly valued in the wider industry, where headhunting is common. Transfers of expertise and drugs between divisions are widespread.**

Which THREE of the following are the most important potential issues that XYZ may encounter due to the divisional structure?

A Autonomy

B Lack of goal congruence

C Growth

D Maintaining a record of movement of goods and services between divisions

E De-motivation

F Devising fair and motivational divisional performance measures

42 **The Finance Director of Huron plc – a large, complex organisation – is considering changing its system for transfer pricing.**

Identify which THREE of the following issues the FD should consider, when considering what criteria a good transfer pricing policy should meet?

A It should provide motivation for divisional managers.

B It should be cheap to run.

C Transfer pricing policy doesn't matter as it is only moving resources between internal SBU's.

D It should allow divisional autonomy and independence to be maintained.

E It should allow divisional performance to be assessed objectively.

43 **Division X of James Ltd is considering a project which will increase annual net profit after tax by £30,000, but will require average inventory levels to increase by £200,000. The current target return on investment is 13% and the imputed interest cost of capital is 12%.**

In these circumstances would the performance evaluation system's return on investment (ROI) and residual income (RI) motivate the managers of division X to act in the interests of the company as a whole?

	ROI	RI
A	Yes	Yes
B	Yes	No
C	No	Yes
D	No	No

$$\frac{30000}{200000} = 15\%$$

$$30000 - (200000 \times 12\%)$$

$$= 6000$$

44   Nova plc is a large, decentralised organisation with 20 divisions. Divisional managers are currently assessed using divisional return on investment (ROI) set against a company-wide target of 15%. Unfortunately the Board have found a number of instances where divisional managers have made decisions that improve their ROI but have eroded shareholder value.

Which TWO of the following proposals will have the best chance of rectifying this situation?

A   Sack all divisional managers that are subsequently found to have eroded shareholder value as this should encourage the others to think more from a company perspective.

B   Set targets based on Economic Value Added (EVA^{TM}) rather than ROI.

C   Set targets based on Residual income (RI) and ROI.

D   Offer divisional managers share options as part of their remuneration package to ensure goal congruence.

E   Insist that all projects are assessed using NPV and set monthly targets based on cash flow rather than profit.

45   Division D of Erie Ltd is considering a project which will increase annual profit by $15,000, but will require average receivables levels to increase by $100,000. The company's target return on investment is 10%, and the imputed interest cost of capital is 9%. Division D currently earns a return on investment of 16%.

Would the return on investment (ROI) and Residual Income (RI) performance measures motivate the manager of Division D to act in the interest of Erie Ltd as a whole?

A   The ROI would motivate the manager to act in the interest of the company as a whole, but the RI would not.

B   The RI would motivate the manager to act in the interest of the company as a whole, but the ROI would not.

C   Both the ROI and the RI would motivate the manager to act in the interest of the company as a whole.

D   Neither the ROI nor the RI would motivate the manager to act in the interest of the company as a whole.

46   TM plc makes components which it sells internally to its subsidiary RM Ltd, as well as to its own external market. The external market price is $24.00 per unit, which yields a contribution of 40% of sales. For external sales, variable costs include $1.50 per unit for distribution costs, which are not incurred on internal sales.

TM plc has sufficient capacity to meet all of the internal and external sales. The objective is to maximise group profit.

At what unit price should the component be transferred to RM Ltd?

A $1.50

B $12.90

C $14.40

D $24.00

47 **Muddy plc has two divisions, A and B, which manufacture bicycles.**

Division A produces the bicycle frames, and Division B assembles the bicycles components onto the frame. There is an external market for both the frames and an external market for the final product.

Both divisions are profit centres. The transfer price for the frame Division A produces has been set at the long term average market price. The following data are available for each division for the Coyote model:

- Estimated selling price for final product   £300
- Long term selling price for frame Division A   £200
- Incremental costs for completion in Division B   £150
- Incremental costs in Division A   £120

The divisional management in B has made the following calculations:

- Selling price for final product   £300
- Less: Transferred- in market costs   £200
- Incremental costs for completion   £150
- Contribution on final product   £(50)

Which ONE of the following statements is TRUE for Muddy plc for the Coyote model?

A   If there are capacity constraints, then in order to maximise return, Division A should satisfy its external market first, then transfer to Division B.

B   Muddy fox should cease production of Coyote bicycles.

C   It doesn't matter what Division A charges Division B.

D   If there are capacity constraints, then in order to maximise return, Division A should transfer frames to Division B before looking to sell frames externally.

48 **Which THREE of the following are drawbacks of using the Balanced Scorecard (BS) model?**

A   The BS does not provide a single view of performance which can lead to confusion.

B   There is no clear link between the balanced scorecard and shareholder analysis.

C   The BS mainly focuses on short-term measures, leading to long-term problems.

D   The BS forces each division within an organisation to use identical indicators.

E   Measures within the BS can conflict with each other, leading to confusion.

49 Alpha and Beta are two divisions of a company. Alpha manufactures two products, X and Y. X is sold outside the company. Y is sold only to division Beta at a unit transfer price of £88. Unit costs for product Y are

	£
Direct materials	30
Direct labour	20
Variable overhead	20
Fixed overhead	10
	80

Division Beta has received an offer from another company to supply a substitute for Y for £76 per unit.

Assuming division Alpha is only operating at 80% of capacity, if Beta accepts the offer the effect on profits will be

	Division Alpha profit	Overall Company profit
A	Decrease	Decrease
B	Increase	Decrease
C	Decrease	Increase
D	Increase	Increase

50 Decentralized organizations can delegate authority and still maintain control and monitor managers' performance by designing appropriate management control system

Which of the following responsibility centres would be evaluated similar to an independent business?

A Profit centre

B Revenue centre

C Investment centre

D Discretionary cost centre

51 Which of the following statements is (are) true regarding managerial decisions?

A The design and use of management control systems affects how an individual makes and implements decisions.

B Rational managers will always make decisions that are in the best interest of the organisation employing them.

A Only A is true

B Only B is true

C Both A and B are true

D Neither A nor B is true

52   Global Stores Inc ('GS') is a large multinational retailer famous for its low prices and high value for money. GS has subsidiaries in many different countries and tax jurisdictions and uses transfer pricing to manage its global tax liability. GS and other global companies are coming under increasing criticism in Country E for paying no corporation tax despite revenues exceeding $50 million. Questions have been asked in parliament and the Government of E is now considering changing its tax rules or even imposing a special super tax on prime offenders.

Identify the best response to the criticism:

A   Release a press statement highlighting the fact that GS is doing nothing illegal and, by saving tax, is creating benefits for its shareholders, staff and customers.

B   Ignore the criticism as most customers will be more interested in GS's lower prices than its record on taxation.

C   Make a large donation to a high profile charity in Country E, ensuring it receives maximum publicity as a result.

D   Open discussions with the tax authorities of Country E to negotiate a fairer system of transfer pricing where it pays tax in E without massively increasing global tax liabilities.

53   Having attended a recent conference on the benefits of Big Data, the Marketing Director of YFT plc, an online retailer, has increased the number of sources it uses to gather information about customers in order to target them with appropriate advertisements and offers. His main concern is that, with so many different sources, there is an increased risk of inaccuracies and hence poor targeting.

Which ONE aspect of Gartner's 4Vs model is the Director having difficulties with?

A   Veracity

B   Velocity

C   Volume

D   Variety

54   J is a senior manager at a hospital. Currently, eye surgeons perform an average of 3 operations per day and this has left the hospital with a sizeable waiting list for such operations. J wishes to raise this to 5 per day. While he is not offering surgeons a bonus for achieving this new level of performance, he is sure that, as it will benefit patients, they will happily accept the new targets.

J has announced the new targets to his surgeons, who were annoyed as J had not previously consulted them about this issue. Privately most surgeons have admitted that they could reach 4 operations per day if they hurried through more routine procedures.

Which ONE of the following problems is J most likely to face with the new targets?

A   Surgeons will see the targets as unachievable and thus become demotivated by them.

B   Surgeons will rush operations, leading to poorer outcomes for patients and damage to the hospital's reputation.

C   Surgeons will demand that they will only work towards the new targets if they receive bonuses.

D   Surgeons will ignore the targets and do as they have always done.

55   Five years ago, PJ chose to compete on the basis of differentiation and so created a set of performance measures for its employees based on high quality production processes. However, the market has now changed and PJ is aware that it needs to lower its cost base to compete with new rivals entering its market. PJ has attempted to change its key performance measures, but has met with significant resistance from staff.

According to Berry, Broadbent and Otley, which ONE of the following problems with performance management systems is PJ experiencing?

A   Gaming

B   Sub-optimisation

C   Ossification

D   Tunnel-vision

56   Which THREE of the following are the most important pre-conditions for the successful implementation of Just-in-Time (JiT) systems? (Select ALL correct answers)

A   Predictable demand

B   Flexible manufacturing systems

C   Price stability

D   Co-operation of suppliers

E   Small batch quantities

57   The 'costs of quality' can be categorised under four headings. Match each cost with the appropriate category.

Category	
Prevention costs	1
Appraisal costs	2
Internal failure costs	3
External failure costs	4

Cost	
Re-working rejected output	3
Customer returns	4
Quality circles	1
Inspection of finished goods	2

58   Managers need to choose information system to support business strategies. Classify the following descriptions using the types of system given:

Description	
These systems handle large volumes of operational-level data, and support structured decision making.	2
These systems allow any user with basic training to make semi-structured or unstructured decisions.	3
These systems allow senior managers to make strategic level decisions.	1

Type of system	
Executive information	1
Management information	
Decision support	
Transaction processing	2
Expert	3

59   Many organisations set up a 'steering committee' to oversee systems development. The purpose of a steering committee is to do which of the following? (Select ALL correct answers)

A   Manage projects

B   Develop new systems

C   Consider the competitive issues raised by IT

D   Plan for new systems

E   Ensure that systems projects achieve the goals of the organisation

60   When a new information system is being developed, or an existing system revised, such development should be carefully controlled.

Which of the following are examples of system development controls? (Select ALL correct answers)

A   System testing

B   Training

C   Formal authorisation of system design

D   System documentation

E   Passwords

61   X is a multi-site organisation, formed by the recent merger of five organisations. Each site currently uses a different information system for the recording and processing of raw material inventory. It is planned to replace these systems with one new system that will be common to every site.

Which of the following system changeover methods may be used? (Select ALL correct answers)

A   Direct

B   Parallel

C   Pilot

D   Phased

62   Direct changeover is assumed to be the highest risk alternative available.

Which TWO of the following controls can mitigate the risk of system failure during direct changeover

A   Testing

B   Training

C   System documentation

D   Data backup

E   Check digits

B2: ETHICAL ISSUES FACING AN ORGANISATION

63   The CIMA Code of Ethics contains five fundamental principles of professional ethics for management accountants. Which of the following are fundamental principles, according to the Code? (Select ALL correct answers)

   A   Confidentiality

   B   Honesty

   C   Objectivity

   D   Respect

   E   Integrity

64   Which THREE of the following are valid reasons for disclosing commercially sensitive information to a third party which would NOT breach the ethical principle of confidentiality?

   A   It is required due to a professional, ethical dilemma

   B   It is permitted by law and authorised by the client

   C   It is required by law

   D   Failure to disclose could materially disadvantage the third party

   E   There is a professional duty or right to disclose the information

65   John is a CIMA Member in Practice, and advises a range of individual clients and organisations. John has been asked by a client to write to one of the client's customers, threatening to report them to the tax authorities if they do not pay a debt due to John's client.

   To do this would be in breach of which fundamental ethical principle (according to CIMA's Code of Ethics)?

   A   integrity

   B   objectivity

   C   professional competence and due care

   D   confidentiality

   E   professional behaviour

66   Graham is a CIMA Member in Practice, and advises a range of individual clients and organisations. Graham has been asked, by his sister, to prepare her tax return. Graham's sister has offered to share any reduction in tax, compared to what she paid last year.

   To do this would be in breach of which fundamental ethical principle (according to CIMA's Code of Ethics)?

   A   integrity

   B   objectivity

   C   professional competence and due care

   D   confidentiality

   E   professional behaviour

67 Peter is a CIMA Member in Practice, and advises a range of individual clients and organisations. Peter has not carried out any Continuing Professional Development (CPD) activity for five years.

This is in breach of which fundamental ethical principle (according to CIMA's Code of Ethics)?

A   integrity

B   objectivity

C   professional competence and due care

D   confidentiality

E   professional behaviour

68 Gregor is a CIMA Member in Practice, and advises a range of individual clients and organisations. Gregor has been asked, by a prospective new client, to divulge details of another client's business activities.

To do this would be in breach of which fundamental ethical principle (according to CIMA's Code of Ethics)?

A   integrity

B   objectivity

C   professional competence and due care

D   confidentiality

E   professional behaviour

69 CIMA's Code of Ethics recommends a four-step process to resolve any ethical conflict. Identify the correct sequence for those steps.

Refuse to remain associated with the conflict	4
Check the facts	1
Escalate externally	3
Escalate internally	2

70 John is a CIMA member, working as Financial Controller of a listed public company. John has shares in the company, and knows that the share price depends to some extent on the reported profits. John is responsible for producing the published accounts of the company.

According to CIMA's Code of Ethics, which TYPE of ethical threat does this represent?

A   self interest

B   self review

C   advocacy

D   intimidation

E   familiarity

71   Gemma is a CIMA member, working as Financial Controller of a listed public company.

The company is in the process of applying for additional loan finance. Gemma has been asked to write to the company's bank, providing a forecast of future cash flows which she knows to be very optimistic. .

According to CIMA's Code of Ethics, which TYPE of ethical threat does this represent?

A   self interest

B   self review

C   advocacy

D   intimidation

E   familiarity

B3: CORPORATE GOVERNANCE

72   Which one of the following is NOT a benefit of corporate governance?

A   Improved access to capital markets

B   Stimulation of performance

C   Enhanced marketability of goods and services

D   Prevention of fraudulent claims by contractors

73   The 'agency problem' refers to which of the following situations?

A   Shareholders acting in their own short-term interests rather than the long-term interests of the company.

B   A vocal minority of shareholders expecting the directors to act as their agents and pay substantial dividends.

C   Companies reliant upon substantial government contracts such that they are effectively agents of the government.

D   The directors acting in their own interests rather than the shareholders' interests.

74   Which TWO of the following are functions of audit committees?

1   Planning the annual external audit.

2   Reviewing the effectiveness of internal financial controls.

3   Reviewing and monitoring the external auditor's independence.

4   Processing year end journal adjustments to the financial statements.

A   1 and 2

B   1 and 3

C   2 and 4

D   2 and 3

75   Which of the following is the main reason for the roles of the chairman and chief executive to be held by different people?

A   To ensure that there is more than one person overseeing the organisation.

B   To ensure decision making power is not concentrated in the hands of one individual.

C   To ensure the CEO can manage staff whilst the chairman meets potential investors.

76   The UK Corporate Governance regime recommends that large listed companies should form an Audit Committee consisting of independent non-executive directors. The Audit Committee should be responsible for which of the following? (Select ALL correct answers)

A   Carrying out internal audit activities

B   Managing internal audit activities

C   Recommending appointment, or removal of the company's external auditor

D   Reviewing the company's system of internal financial controls

E   Carrying out external audit activities

77   The UK Corporate Governance regime recommends that large listed companies should form a Remuneration Committee. The Remuneration Committee should be responsible for which of the following? (Select ALL correct answers)

A   Setting the remuneration level of the Executive Directors

B   Setting the remuneration level of the Chairman

C   Recommending on the remuneration level of the Senior Managers

D   Setting the remuneration level of the Non-Executive Directors

E   Setting the remuneration level of the External Auditor

78   The remuneration committee of Ghee plc, a listed company, consists of 4 Directors with the HR Director chairing the committee. The other three members are NED's although only one of these has been assessed as independent by the nominations committee. The remuneration committee has responsibility for both executive and non-executive pay policy with these policies being put forward by approval at the AGM by shareholders.

What actions should Ghee take to comply with best practice corporate governance? Select ALL that apply.

A   HR Director should resign from Ghee

B   HR director should resign from the chairman position of the remuneration committee

C   Non-independent NED should resign from the remuneration committee

D   Remuneration committee should not have responsibility for NED remuneration

E   All NEDs on remuneration committee should be replaced

79   Monk plc, a listed entity, currently has a governance structure that consists of an Executive Chairman, who acts as both Chairman and CEO, together with 4 executive directors and 1 non-executive director. What would you recommend in order for Monk plc to comply with best practice corporate governance?

   A   Removing the non-executive director as he/she is unlikely to have much knowledge of the business due to a lack of day to day involvement.

   B   Creating a separate role for chairman and CEO to replace the current role of Executive Chairman, recruiting an independent person for the position of chairman and recruiting additional non-executive directors to create a more balanced board.

   C   Replacing the role of Executive Chairman with the post of CEO and recruiting additional non-executive directors to create a more balanced board.

80   Which of the following does NOT represent good corporate governance?

   A   Membership of the audit committee should include at least three non-executive directors.

   B   Ensuring that non-executive directors do not participate at board meetings.

   C   Segregation between the roles of chairman and chief executive officer.

   D   At least one member of the audit committee should have recent, relevant financial experience.

81   Which of the following remuneration package elements for Directors will best ensure goal congruence between the interests of shareholders and executive directors?

   A   Cash bonus paid to directors if the company achieves profit growth targets.

   B   Cash bonus paid if directors achieve a range of individual performance related targets linked to the balanced scorecard.

   C   Share option bonus scheme that is paid if the company achieves profit growth targets.

   D   Private Health insurance for directors and their immediate family.

INTERNAL CONTROLS TO MANAGE RISK

C1: CONTROL SYSTEMS

82   Information system controls can be classified as either general, application, software or network controls.

   Match the examples below to the appropriate category.

Category	
General	1
Application	2
Software	3
Network	4

Example	
Licenses	3
Check digits	2
Anti-virus software	4
Passwords	1

83   Information system controls can be classified as either general, application, software or network controls.

Match the examples below to the appropriate category.

Category	
General 2	
Application 1	
Software 3	
Network 4	

Example	
Firewalls 4	
Training 2	
Pre-numbered forms 1	
Licenses 3	

84   Information system controls can be classified as 'security controls' and 'integrity controls'. Drag and drop the following controls into the correct category.

	Security	Integrity
Locked doors	✓	
Passwords	✓	
Batch totals		✓
Reconciliation		✓
CCTV	✓	
Check digits		✓
Authorisation of data entry	✓	
Fire alarms	✓	

85   The Data Protection Act contains eight 'data protection principles'. Identify which of the following are data protection principles. (Select ALL correct answers)

A   Personal data shall be confirmed with the data subject.

B   Personal data shall be accurate and kept up to date.

C   A data subject is responsible for the security and protection of data.

D   A data subject is entitled to access and to have data corrected or erased.

E   Personal data shall be held and used only for specified purposes.

86   The Data Protection Act covers a wide range of information systems. Identify which of the following are exempt from one or more of the principles of the Act. (Select ALL correct answers)

A   Bank records

B   Manual records

C   Medical records

D   Payroll records

E   Crime records

87   **DF plc has identified a critical success factor (CSF) for its organisation:**

'Having an excellent quality product.'

Which ONE of the following would be the most suitable key performance indicator for this CSF?

A   Reduce the number of defects identified by quality control and customers by 15%.

B   Reduce the average time taken to deal with complaints about quality by 10%.

C   Increase quality by 50% over the next year.

D   Increase the amount of quality training for production staff.

88   **S is a recently qualified Management Accountant who has just started working at Bob Ltd, a small building firm based in the UK.**

One of S's duties is to oversee the internal controls of the company. However S is not sure how far her remit extends, as she is unsure what is covered by the term 'internal controls'

Which ONE would best describe the broad term of internal controls

A   A financial restriction place on the company.

B   An activity, which has been ordered to be completed by the auditors of a company.

C   An activity, which is in place to control certain risks and to help an organisation achieve its objectives.

D   An activity the human resources department conducts to ensure all employees are doing their job correctly.

89   **SSS plc is a supermarket based in the UK and another European country. SSS's internal auditor has indentified the following risks and internal controls to reduce those risks**

Reconcile the FOUR risks to the FOUR internal controls.

Internal Controls		Risks	
A	Prepare and reconcile budget to actual spend 1	1	The risk of overspending on a construction project
B	Hedging techniques 4	2	The risk of employees stealing products
C	Tight stock control systems 3	3	The risk of obsolescence, due to items with a short period of consumption
D	CCTV cameras in store 2	4	The risk of exchange rate fluctuation between Stirling and the Euro.

90   **Which TWO of the following are objectives of the controls in the revenue cycle?**

1   Goods are only supplied to customers who pay promptly and in full

2   All purchases are made with reliable and competitively priced suppliers

3   Orders are despatched promptly and in full to the correct customer

4   Only genuine employees are paid

A   1 and 2

B   1 and 3

C   2 and 3

D   3 and 4

91 **Which TWO of the following are objectives of the controls in the payroll cycle?**

    1   Expenditure is recorded accurately and related payables are recorded at an appropriate value.

    2   All purchases and related payables are recorded.

    3   Correct amounts owed are recorded and paid to the taxation authorities.

    4   Employees are paid at the correct rate of pay.

    A   1 and 2

    B   1 and 3

    C   2 and 3

    D   3 and 4

92 **Which TWO of the following controls in a purchase cycle could be implemented to reduce the risk of payment of goods not received?**

    1   Sequentially pre-numbered purchase requisitions and sequence check.

    2   Matching of goods received note with purchase invoice.

    3   Goods are inspected for condition and quantity and agreed to purchase order before acceptance.

    4   Daily update of inventory system.

    A   1 and 2

    B   2 and 3

    C   2 and 4

    D   3 and 4

93 **Which TWO of the following controls in the purchase cycle could be implemented to reduce the risk of procurement of unnecessary goods and services?**

    1   Centralised purchasing department.

    2   Sequentially pre-numbered purchase requisitions and sequence check.

    3   Orders can only be placed with suppliers from the approved suppliers list.

    4   All purchase requisitions are signed as authorised by an appropriate manager.

    A   1 and 3

    B   1 and 4

    C   2 and 4

    D   3 and 4

94   X is a manufacturing company. It makes one product, the Y. The quality inspectors of X currently reject 3% of the finished Ys produced, as they are unfit for purpose. Which of the following controls should reduce the rejection rate? (Select ALL correct answers)

A   Increased training of quality inspectors

B   Increased training of production staff

C   Purchasing higher quality raw materials

D   Better finished goods inventory handling procedures

E   Employing more quality inspectors

95   X is a retailer. It currently suffers significant losses due to theft by staff and customers. Which of the following controls should reduce the number of thefts? (Select ALL correct answers)

A   Employing more security guards

B   Improving staff selection procedures

C   Reducing inventory levels

D   Installing CCTV systems in stores

E   Making suppliers responsible for the cost of thefts

C2: RISK MANAGEMENT STRATEGIES AND INTERNAL CONTROLS

96   The following are all types of control within an organisation:

(i)   Logical access controls

(ii)   Database controls

(iii)   Hierarchical passwords

(iv)   Range checks

Which of the above controls help to ensure the security of highly confidential information?

A   (i) and (ii) only

B   (i) and (iii) only

C   (i), (ii) and (iii) only

D   All of the above

97   Foney Ltd has recently experienced a downturn in sales of their own-brand Vodka. The Marketing Director has approached the board of directors with his idea to reinvigorate the sales demand. He has suggested that the company invests in new packaging and re-brand the Vodka to look exactly like a leading well-known brand of vodka, even using their name but selling the product to small off licenses for half the price charged by the market leader.

Which for the ONE following courses of actions would you suggest to the Board of Foney Ltd and why?

A   Implement the Marketing Director's idea as it makes strategic sense.

B   Do not proceed as it is too costly.

C   Do not proceed as the situation described by the Marketing Director is counterfeiting.

D   Do not proceed as the situation described by the Marketing Director is embezzlement.

98   Jack, a CIMA member, has recently taken a fantastic position as finance manager for a medium-sized fashion retail company, Acia clothing plc. Jack really enjoys the job and even though the remuneration is not great, the other managers at the company have explained the way they 'get around' that issue. The sales manager explains to Jack that the key is to 'put everything on expenses – private petrol, drinks and even clothing, It's all fine and as long as you have a receipt, no-one in the finance department will question it'. He continues that 'It's fine because the board are aware of it and turn a blind eye'.

Which ONE of the following essential internal control measures is evidently missing from this company?

A   Acia lacks a control environment, Acia are without a board setting an ethical tone at the top

B   Acia lacks an Internal Audit department

C   Acia lacks an experienced finance manager

D   Acia lacks an external auditor

99   Silvermans plc, a large investment bank, has just been involved in a highly publicised fraud investigation concerning the secretary of the Board of Directors.

The investigation found that the secretary had managed to steal £2 million from the directors after they had entrusted her with their chequebooks to settle all personal and professional financial affairs. Within a year the secretary was forging the directors' signatures and transferring monies into her private account

Which ONE of the three prerequisites for fraud had the bosses allowed to flourish within this situation?

A   Rationalisation

B   Motive

C   Greed

D   Opportunity

100 Fraud risk, such as false accounting or theft of cash or assets, is one component of which type of risk?

A   Strategic risk

B   Operational risk

C   Financial risk

D   All of above

101 The Finance Director of X plc recently attended a CPD seminar entitled 'Fraud – How to design an anti-fraud strategy'. Her original understanding of her fiduciary duty regarding fraud was that it was her job to detect any wrong doing. However the seminar enabled her to understand there are other aspects to an anti-fraud strategy.

Which of the following components are key to an effective anti-fraud strategy (select ALL that apply)?

A   Prevention

B   Deterrence

C   Response

D   Control

102 Aggrico Bank plc has just employed a new Chief Executive Officer (CEO) after the departing Chief was convicted of a high level fraud. The new CEO has said that she is committed to developing a sound ethical culture to ensure the long-term survival of the bank.

Which of the following policies would help the new CEO to achieve her aim? (select ALL that apply)

A   Establish clear anti-fraud policy statements, with explanations about acceptable behaviour.

B   A process of reminders to employees regarding fraud policy.

C   A large redundancy process with removes long-standing employee from the bank.

D   Establish a route through which suspected fraud can be reported.

103 The primary responsibility for the prevention and detection of fraud rests with which ONE stakeholder group?

A   The Board of Directors

B   The internal auditors

C   The external auditors

D   The Non-Executive Directors

104 Rural Ltd is an independent, small, family-owned construction business that has seen a period of rapid expansion and growth over the last five years. Until now the family have simply relied on informal trust based control systems. However, the finance officer has started to see small inventory discrepancies, the bank reconciliation not quite reconciling and he also suspects internal leaks of client information to a leading competitor.

Which of the following internal control policies would be appropriate for Rural Ltd. to implement? (Select ALL that apply)

A   Fit CCTV cameras in stockrooms

B   Requiring the division of responsibility within the purchasing process – one employee to order goods but another to authorise payment

C   Restricting personal USB drives from being brought into the office environment

D   Calling the National Crime Agency (NCA)

105 X is a hospital. In the past six months, three of the hospital staff have been attacked when walking home from work late at night. Which of the following controls should reduce the number of attacks? (Select ALL correct answers)

A   Giving all members of staff mobile telephones to report attacks

B   Providing a free bus service for staff finishing work late at night

C   Taking out insurance against attacks on staff

D   Changing the shift pattern, so staff end their shift during daylight

E   Installing floodlighting in the hospital grounds and car parks

106 H has been offering investors in his company a 15% per annum return on their investment. In order to fund this return, H has been using money raised from newer investors to pay the 15% returns demanded by early investors.

What type of fraud is H committing?

A   Manipulation of revenue recognition

B   Advance fee fraud

C   False billing fraud

D   Ponzi scheme

107 BNG Ltd has recently discovered that it has been the victim of a false-billing fraud. Which of the following controls could BNG put in place to prevent this from occurring in the future?

A   Segregation of duties within the accounts department

B   Regular receivables ledger reconciliations

C   Authorisation of payments by management

D   Maintenance of a regular trial balance

108 **Fredrickson and Co is a consultancy company that has recently seen the CEO forced to tender her resignation over serious fraud allegations. The rest of the board are looking to regain shareholder confidence.**

Identify the THREE main fraud prevention strategies you would recommend to the Board.

A Create and publish a whistle blowing policy

B No nothing, as most shareholders will probably be uninterested

C Create a sound system of internal control

D Create a culture that is anti-fraud with an anti-fraud 'tone at the top'

E Announce a special dividend to be paid to all shareholders

F Dismiss any employee who directly reported to the CEO just in case they might have been involved in any wrong doing

C3: INTERNAL AUDIT

109 **Many organisations consider outsourcing their Internal Audit function. Which of the following are ADVANTAGES of doing this? (Select ALL correct answers)**

A Specialist skills may be more readily available

B Risk of staff turnover is passed to the outsourcing firm

C Better understanding of the organisation's objectives and culture

D May improve independence

E Decisions relating to Internal Audit can be based solely on cost

110 **Many organisations consider outsourcing their Internal Audit function. Which of the following are DISADVANTAGES of doing this? (Select ALL correct answers)**

A Flexibility and availability may not be as high as with an in-house function

B Decisions relating to Internal Audit may be based solely on cost

C Increased management time

D Possible conflict of interest if provided by the external auditors

E Loss of control over standard of service

111 **Internal and external audit have similarities, but several features distinguish between them.**

Drag and drop the following distinguishing features into the correct category.

	Internal Audit	External Audit
Required by shareholders	✓	
Required by statute		✓
Reports to Shareholders and Management		✓
Reports to Audit Committee or Directors	✓	
Reports on financial statements		✓
Reports on controls	✓	

112 Jan has been invited to run her company's first Internal Audit department. Jan is currently discussing plans for the department with the Finance Director, who is Jan's existing line manager. The Finance Director has made a number of suggestions but Jan is worried they might contravene Internal Audit Attribute Standards.

For each suggestion identify which Internal Audit Attribute Standards are being contravened, if any:

Suggestion	Internal Audit Attribute Standard contravened
It should not be a problem that Jan has no experience of audit and is only part-qualified. *1*	Independence *3*
The first project for the new department should be to audit the Treasury Department, which Jan currently manages. *2*	Objectivity *2*
Jan, as Head of Internal Audit, should report to the Finance Director. *3*	Professional Care *1*
	None contravened

113 Portland plc has a well-established internal audit department consisting of staff that have an average length of service of six years. The scope of the internal auditors work is determined by the Chief Financial Officer (CFO). For some projects the internal audit teams review their own work.

Which of the following statements are correct?

1   The independence of the internal audit department could be enhanced if another member of the finance team was involved in determining the scope of their work.

2   To eliminate any self-review threats Portland plc could increase expenditure on training so that internal auditors are better able to identify errors in their own work.

3   Staff should be rotated on a regular basis to reduce the familiarity threat associated with the long length of service.

A   Both 1 and 2

B   2 only

C   Both 1 and 3

D   3 only

114 FTS plc is planning to introduce a new benchmarking procedure as part of internal audit to help identify risk areas but is unsure which type of benchmarking would be most appropriate. It is aware that each type of benchmarking has certain drawbacks.

FTS has identified that _____1_____ benchmarking is often difficult to undertake as it is difficult to convince the other party to share information about their operations.

_____2_____ benchmarking is unlikely to suggest any strategic risks for the whole organisation and is typically only useful where the organisation feels that conformity of service is crucial to its operations.

Finally, _____3_____ benchmarking often fails to provide data on the benchmarking company's core functions as it requires the organisation to benchmark itself against an organisation in a different industry.

Use the options below to fill in the missing words in gaps 1, 2 and 3.

A   Process

B   Internal

C   Competitive

115 Which of the following is an example of an analytical review procedure?

    A   Comparing gross profit margin to the prior year figure to identify significant changes

    B   Enquiries of management regarding the risks of the business

    C   Observation of internal control procedures

    D   Recalculation of a balance

116 Moyles Co operate a chain of car dealerships and has a large internal audit department in place. The management of Moyles Co are keen to increase the range of assignments that internal audit undertake.

Which TWO of the following assignments could the internal audit department of Moyles Co be asked to perform by management?

    1   Fill a temporary vacancy in the credit control department on a rotational basis.

    2   Under the external auditor's supervision, assist the external auditors by evaluating returns from the receivables circularisation.

    3   Implement a new inventory control system.

    4   Evaluate the inventory count instructions.

    A   1 and 2

    B   3 and 4

    C   2 and 4

    D   1 and 3

117 **Carson plc is a small family-run company selling fishing tackle and bait from a small chain of shops. The firm has seen rapid sales growth since engaging in e-commerce via a website and selling via large online auction sites.**

The newly appointed Finance Director is the only Board member from outside the family and has suggested it would be a good idea for Carson plc to consider establishing an internal audit department as he has already noticed a large inventory discrepancy for fishing clothing.

Which THREE of the following factors are the main reasons for the need for an internal audit at Carson plc?

A   The fact the board has majority family members

B   If a company is listed on the stock exchange it must have an internal audit

C   The growing scale and variety of selling channels suggests there is a higher risk of error

D   Potential internal control issues are starting to arise

E   The introduction of e-commerce

F   The wish of shareholders

118 **B retail has discovered that staff have been excessively discounting stock for sale to friends and family at 2 stores. This is against B retail's staff policies and procedures. They would like their internal audit department to look into this issue at their other 25 stores.**

Which of the following types of audit would be applicable? (select ALL that apply)

A   Compliance audit

B   Management audit

C   Systems audit

D   Risk based audit

E   Environmental audit

119 **Which of the systems below would be audited as a "systems-based audit"?**

A   Sales ledger system

B   EPOS (Electronic point of sale) system

C   Non-current asset recording

D   All of the above

120 **Once an audit is completed an audit report is issued. Which of the following are appropriate features of an audit report? (Select ALL that apply)**

A   Recommendations for action

B   Audit opinion/grading of the area/system reviewed

C   Results of tests carried out

D   Objectives of the audit

E   Summary of the audit process for this audit

MANAGING RISKS ASSOCIATED WITH CASH FLOWS

D1: EVALUATE FINANCIAL RISKS FACING AN ORGANISATION.

121 **For which of the following reasons do exchange rates fluctuate? (Select ALL correct answers)**

A   Changes in the balance of payments

B   Government policy

C   Developments in Information Technology

D   Speculation

E   Capital movements between economies

122 **'There is a risk that the value of our foreign currency-denominated assets and liabilities will change when we prepare our accounts.'**

To which risk does the above statement refer?

A   Translation risk

B   Economic risk

C   Transaction risk

D   Interest rate risk

123 **Eady plc is a UK company that imports furniture from a Canadian supplier and sells it throughout Europe. Eady plc has just received a shipment of furniture, invoiced in Canadian dollars, for which payment is to be made in two months' time. Neither Eady plc nor the Canadian supplier use hedging techniques to cover their exchange risk.**

If the pound sterling were to weaken substantially against the Canadian dollar, what would be the foreign exchange gain or loss effects upon Eady plc and the Canadian supplier?

	Eady plc	Canadian supplier
A	Gain	No effect
B	No effect	Gain
C	Loss	No effect
D	Loss	Gain

124 **In periods of rising inflation, commodities can act as a hedge to a portfolio of shares and bonds because the:**

A   Commodities will not be affected by a rise in inflation.

B   Commodities will typically appreciate in price when prices of stocks and bonds decline.

C   Commodities can provide current income to offset any price decreases in shares and bonds.

D   Decreases in price of commodities.

125 **The interest rate risk of a bond is the:**

    A   risk related to the possibility of bankruptcy of the bond's issuer.

    B   unsystematic risk caused by factors unique in the bond.

    C   risk related to the possibility of bankruptcy of the bond's issuer, that arises from the uncertainty of the bond's return caused by the change in interest rates.

    D   risk that arises from the uncertainty about the bond's return caused by changes in interest rates over time.

126 **Political risk analysis is conducted by a company considering international operations and normally focuses on the:**

    A   world economy generally

    B   relations between the USA, Japan and Europe

    C   political and cultural differences between the home and target country

    D   industrialisation of the target country

127 **When using the expected value criterion, it is assumed that the individual wants to**

    A   maximise return for a given level of risk

    B   maximise return irrespective of the level of risk

    C   minimise risk for a given level of return

    D   minimise risk irrespective of the level of return

128 **A company has constructed a model for predicting profits. Net profit or loss depends on two variables: gross profit and overheads. The following are independent probability distributions of the two variables.**

Gross profit	Probability	Overheads	Probability
12,000	0.1	6,000	0.3
6,000	0.4	4,000	0.3
4,000	0.4	3,000	0.3
3,000	0.1	2,000	0.1

What is the probability that the company will make a positive net profit?

    A   0.27

    B   0.55

    C   0.73

    D   0.82

129   Joe is supervisor of the Receivables Team at X Ltd. He has been told that he is responsible for managing 'credit risk'.

Identify which THREE of the following directly determine the level of credit risk to which X is exposed.

A   The total volume of sales

B   The total volume of credit sales

C   The time allowed to customers to pay

D   Debt collection procedures

E   Joe's management style

130   Company P has decided to finance its foreign investment through local finance. Which of the following statements is correct? (Select all that apply)

A   Local financing can minimise translation risk

B   Local financing can minimise transaction risk

C   Local financing can minimise interest rate risk

D   Local financing is dependent on the state of the banking and capital markets of the country concerned

E   Local financing reduces the risk of P's assets being confiscated

D2: EVALUATE ALTERNATIVE RISK MANAGEMENT TOOLS.

EXCHANGE RATE THEORY AND VALUE AT RISK

131   Inflation in the UK is 5%p.a. and in the US is 6%p.a. Given that the spot rate is currently GBP 1 = USD 1.5000, what will a UK company have to pay in Sterling, in 12 months, to buy a commodity costing $10,000 (assuming Purchasing Power Parity)? (Answer to the nearest GBP).

132   Interest rates in the UK are forecast to be 2% over the next year and 3% in the Eurozone. The current spot rate is GBP 1 = EUR 1.25.

Determine the exchange rate in one year (assuming Interest Rate Parity). (Give your answer in the form GBP 1 = EUR... working to 4 dp).

133   Interest Rate Parity Theory generally holds true in practice. However it suffers from several limitations.

Which of the following is not a limitation of Interest Rate Parity Theory?

A   Government controls on capital markets

B   Controls on currency trading

C   Intervention in foreign exchange markets

D   Future inflation rates are only estimates

(handwritten at top: $1+0.1342 = (1+r) \times 1+5\%$ $1.0802 = 1+r$)

134 In Country A inflation is predicted to be 5% and (nominal) interest rates are 11.3%. In Country B interest rates are 13.42%.

Assuming the International Fischer effect holds, determine the expected inflation rate in Country B. (Give your answer as a percentage to 1 decimal place)

135 The current spot exchange rate between sterling and the Euro is EUR 1.4415/GBP. The sterling three month interest rate is 5.75% pa and the Euro three month interest rate is 4.75% pa.

(handwritten: $1.113 = 1+r \times 1+5\%$ $1.1342 = 1+6 \times 1+i$)

What should the three month EUR/GBP forward rate be?

A   1.4553

B   1.4379

C   1.4279   *(handwritten: $1.4415 \times \dfrac{1.0475}{1.0575}$ 1.014375)*

D   1.4451

136 X is a bank. The management accountant of X has estimated that the value of its asset portfolio at year end will be $1,200 million, with a standard deviation of $430 million. Calculate the value at risk of the portfolio, at a 95% confidence level. (Express your answer in $, rounded to the nearest million.)

(handwritten: $430 \times 1.645 = 707.35$)

FOREIGN EXCHANGE RATE RISK MANAGEMENT

137 Edted plc has to pay a Spanish supplier EUR 100,000 in three months' time. The company's Finance Director wishes to avoid exchange rate exposure, and is looking at four options.

(1)   Do nothing for three months and then buy Euros at the spot rate.

(2)   Pay in full now, buying Euros at today's spot rate.

(3)   Buy Euros now, put them on deposit for three months, and pay the debt with these Euros plus accumulated interest.

(4)   Arrange a forward exchange contract to buy the euros in three months' time.

Which of these options would provide cover against the exchange rate exposure that Edted would otherwise suffer?

A   Option (4) only

B   Options (3) and (4) only

C   Options (2), (3) and (4) only

D   Options (1), (2), (3) and (4)

138 Which of the following measures will allow a UK company to enjoy the benefits of a favourable change in exchange rates for their Euro receivables contracts while protecting them from unfavourable exchange rate movements?

(handwritten: Sell = put)

A   A forward exchange contract

B   A put option for Euros

C   A call option for Euros

D   A money market hedge

139 Methods for hedging foreign currency risk can be classified as either 'internal' or 'external'. Drag and drop the following hedging methods into the correct category.

	Internal	External
Forward contracts		✓
Futures		✓
Leading and lagging	✓	
Matching and netting	✓	
Options		✓
Countertrade	✓	

140 There are different methods that can be used to internally hedge foreign exchange risk. Match the examples below to the appropriate method.

Method	Example
Matching 2	Transferring all bank account balances in one currency into a single account 1
Netting 3	Exchanging goods or services of similar value 4
Pooling 1	Financing a foreign investment with a foreign currency loan 2
Countertrade 4	Using a foreign currency receipt to offset a foreign currency payment 3

141 The following options are held by Frances plc at their expiry date:

Call = right to buy

(1) A call option on GBP 500,000 in exchange for USD at an exercise price of GBP 1 = USD 1.90. The exchange rate at the expiry date is GBP 1 = USD 1.95.

Put = right to sell

(2) A put option on GBP 400,000 in exchange for Singapore Dollars at an exercise price of GBP 1 = SGD 2.90. The exchange rate at the expiry date is GBP 1 = SGD 2.95.

Which one of the following combinations (exercise/lapse) should be undertaken by the company?

	Call	*Put*
A	Exercise	Lapse
B	Exercise	Exercise
C	Lapse	Exercise
D	Lapse	Lapse

142 SGB Ltd in the UK have sold USD 5m worth of goods to AW Inc. in the US, they are considering hedging the contract using options.

The current spot is £/$1.5500 and the option strike price is GBP 1 = USD 1.6000 the contract size is GBP 25,000 per contract and the premium is USD 1,000 per contract.

What is the GBP value of the premium that SGB must pay?

A 80,645

B 83,226

C 125,000

D 129,000

143 X (a UK company) has purchased goods for USD 50,000 and payment is due in 30 days. The current spot rate for USD is GBP1/USD 1.5500 – 1.5400 and the one month forward contract is priced at 0.50-0.30 cpm. Calculate the amount of GBP that X will pay under the forward contract (to the nearest GBP).

(handwritten: 1·5400 / 1·537)

144 X (a UK company) must pay EUR 1 million to a Spanish supplier in six months' time. The treasurer of X has obtained the following information:

(handwritten: → 990099)

(handwritten left margin: → 980392)

- Spot rate GBP 1/EUR 1.2000 – 1.1950

(handwritten: 828535)

- EUR borrowing can be obtained at 4.0%p.a. and deposits pay 2.0%p.a.

(handwritten left margin: 816994) *(handwritten: 849248 / 808329)*

- GBP borrowing can be obtained at 5.0%p.a. and deposits pay 3.0%p.a.

(handwritten left margin: 829248)

Calculate the cost to X in GBP of a money market hedge, to the nearest GBP. (Round calculations to the nearest GBP or EUR, at each stage of the calculation).

145 DWTV Inc. a US company has purchased goods from T2 in the UK at a cost of GBP 25 Million. They have taken out an option at a strike price of GBP 1 = 1.6700 USD with a premium of USD 85,000. When the contract is closed out the spot rate is 1.6850.

What is the USD cost of the purchase to DWTV Inc?

(handwritten:
Option   Spot
41·750000   42125000
85000   85000
41835000)

INTEREST RATE RISK MANAGEMENT

146 When hedging interest rate risk, a variety of instruments are available. Match the instruments below with the relevant descriptions.

Instrument		Description	
A	Forward Rate Agreement (FRA) *3*	1	A traded instrument, hedging only downside risk
B	Interest Rate Guarantee (IRG) *4*	2	A traded instrument, with a fixed rate
C	Future *4 2*	3	An over the counter instrument, with a fixed rate
D	Option *1*	4	An over the counter instrument, hedging only downside risk

147 X (a company) wishes to borrow $1 million in three months, for a period of six months. A bank has quoted the following (Forward Rate Agreement) FRA rates:

3 v 9 5.55 – 5.70   *(handwritten: 3 v 9)*

X can borrow at 0.50% above base rate, and the base rate is currently 4.50%. Concerned that base rates may rise, X decides to take the FRA offered by the bank.

At the settlement date for the FRA, base rate has risen to 6.00%. What is the effective interest rate paid by X, for its borrowing? (Answer in %, to 2 decimal places).

148 The owner of an interest-rate cap will *(handwritten: ↓ down   Buy)*

A   receive a payment if the market rate exceeds the cap rate

B   receive a payment if the market rate is less than the cap rate

C   be required to make a payment if the market rate exceeds the cap rate

D   be required to make a payment if the market rate is less than the cap rate

149 **DD Co has a floating rate borrowing with an interest rate of LIBOR + 1.5%.**

The directors are concerned that interest rates are forecast to rise, so they have approached their bank to discuss the possibility of entering an interest rate swap.

The bank has quoted swap rates of 4.9% – 5% against LIBOR.

If DD Co enters the swap arrangement, what net interest rate will it pay?

A   LIBOR + 5%

B   5%

C   6.4%

D   6.5%

150 **Company A would like to take out a variable rate loan for a new project. Company B also has a new project but would like to take out a fixed rate loan in order to have certainty over interest payments.**

Company A has been quoted a fixed rate of 7% and a variable rate of LIBOR + 4%. Company B has been quoted a fixed rate of 6% and a variable rate of LIBOR + 2% as it has a higher credit rating than A.

If they enter into a swap arrangement, agreeing to split gains equally, what effective rate will each end up paying?

A	Co A 7%	Co B	LIBOR + 2%
B	Co A LIBOR + 4%	Co B	6%
C	Co A LIBOR + 2%	Co B	7%
D	Co A LIBOR + 3.5%	Co B	5.5%

151 **Grudem plc needs to borrow USD 12 million in 6 month's time as is concerned about interest rate risk exposure.**

Which of the following strategies would help Grudem manage this risk? (Select ALL that apply).

A   Sell FRAs

B   Buy put options on short term interest rate futures

C   Buy an interest rate cap

D   Buy bond futures

152 **Match how you would calculate the value of the net payment or receipt of interest in each of the following situations:**

Situation	Calculations
Company has a loan and a cap where the strike rate is higher than the market rate	Strike rate + premium costs
Company has a deposit and a floor where the strike rate is higher than the market rate	Market rate + premium costs
Company has a loan and a cap where the strike rate is less than the market rate	Strike rate – premium costs
Company has a deposit and a floor where the strike rate is less than the market rate	Market rate – premium costs

153 **Match which option or combination of options would be needed to achieve the following required risk positions:**

Required position		Combination of options	
A 'cap' on the interest rate on a loan	1	Buy a Put on a FRA and sell a call on a FRA	3
A 'floor' on the interest rate on a deposit	2	Buy a Call on a FRA	2
A 'collar' to protect the interest cost of a loan	4	Buy a Call on a FRA and sell a put on a FRA	4
A 'collar' to protect the interest on a deposit	3	Buy a Put on a FRA	1

154 **An interest rate option is:**

CCC
PDF

A   A right but not an obligation to buy or sell interest rate futures

B   An obligation to obtain a loan at an agreed interest rate at a future date

C   A right but not an obligation to obtain a loan at a future date

D   A right but not an obligation to an agreed interest rate on a notional loan

155 **Which of the following statements are true for an interest rate floor (select ALL that apply):**

A   Can be achieved by buying a call on a FRA

B   Is useful where a company is concerned about the cost of a loan

C   Is useful when interest rates are thought likely to fall

D   Will effectively reduce the interest rate on a deposit because of the premium costs

E   Guarantees the minimum value of a loan

156 **According to the Black-Scholes model, five variables affect the price of a call option.**

Which of the following are components of the Black-Scholes model? (Select ALL correct answers)

A   The spot price of the underlying asset

B   The tax rate

C   The variability of the price of the underlying asset

D   The time to maturity

E   The risk free interest rate

157 **Most futures contracts are closed through which ONE of the following:**

A   delivery

B   arbitrage

C   a reversing trade

D   an exchange-for-physicals

158 Which one of the following statements regarding Over-the-Counter derivatives is true?

- A   They carry no default risk
- B   They are customized contracts
- C   They are backed by the OTC Clearinghouse
- D   They have good liquidity in the over-the-counter (OTC) market

159 Which of the following is least likely to be described as a benefit of derivatives markets?

- A   Derivatives markets help keep interest rates down
- B   Derivatives markets supply valuable price information
- C   Derivatives allow the shifting of risk to those who can most efficiently bear it
- D   Transactions costs are usually smaller in derivatives markets than for similar trades in the underlying asset

160 Pick three advantages of options from the list of properties below:

- A   Provide complete certainty as to the amount to be paid or received
- B   Simple to understand and cheap to operate
- C   Provide a means of hedging uncertain transactions
- D   Guaranteed conformance to hedge accounting requirements
- E   Provide a guaranteed minimum sum received or maximum sum paid
- F   Ensure that the cash flows associated with financing the transaction are known in advance

MANAGING RISKS ASSOCIATED WITH CAPITAL INVESTMENT DECISIONS

E1: INVESTMENT APPRAISAL

161 The Adjusted Present Value (APV) method of project appraisal should be used when capital structure is expected <DROP DOWN BOX> as a result of the project.

- A   not to change
- B   to change a little
- C   to change significantly

162 Which of the following conditions are necessary for a company to use the pre-project company weighted average cost of capital (WACC) as a discount rate for project appraisal? (Select ALL correct answers)

- A   The capital structure will change, as a result of the project
- B   The project carries a different level of business risk from the company's existing operations
- C   The new investment is large, in comparison to the capital of the company
- D   The company will raise additional finance to maintain its current gearing ratio
- E   The WACC is above bank base rate

163 A decision-maker wishes to use certainty equivalents as part of a net present value (NPV) calculation. What is the appropriate discount rate to use in such an approach?

- A   the company's cost of debt
- B   the company's cost of equity
- C   the company's WACC
- D   the risk free rate
- E   the bank base rate

164 SCW plc makes equipment for a range of countryside activities, including camping, hunting, shooting and fishing. It is currently financed purely by equity. The FD is currently assessing four new investment opportunities.

Select the best investment appraisal technique for each of the investment scenarios given (Note: you can choose the same technique more than once if you wish)

Projects	Techniques
A – Develop a new range of light weight crossbows. Finance by cutting the forthcoming dividend. APV	Adjusted Present Value
B – Diversify into making luxury yachts. Finance to be raised to maintain the current gearing ratio. 2	Calculate a NPV using a risk-adjusted WACC 2
C – Develop a new range of weapons for the police force of Country P. SCW can access a subsidized loan as part of the proposal. APV	Calculate a NPV using the existing company WACC as a discount rate 1
D – Building a new range of fly fishing reels. Finance to be raised via a rights issue. 1	

165 The higher risk of a project can be incorporated into investment appraisal by decreasing

- A   The cost of the initial investment of the project
- B   The estimates of future cash inflows from the project
- C   The internal rate of return of the project
- D   The required rate of return of the project

166 Zodhiates plc is looking at different alternatives for building its new factory and has decided to design it around modules with general purpose plant and machinery rather than a more traditional specialised production line.

Which ONE of the following real options is included within the factory decision?

- A   Option to abandon
- B   Option to delay
- C   Option to follow on
- D   Option to return

167 **X (a company) is considering an investment project that requires a $3 million investment. The risk free rate is 8%, and the directors are 95% certain that cash savings will be made in perpetuity.**

Calculate the annual cash saving required for the project to break even. (Answer in $, rounded to the nearest $)

$$3 = \frac{? \times 0.95}{0.08}$$

168 **Which of the following parties is least likely to benefit from capital investment decisions that increase risk and expected return for a company?**

 A Creditors

 B Chief executive officers

 C Chief financial officers

 D Shareholders

169 **Y Ltd is a small, family-owned car sales company, currently financed by a mixture of debt and equity. The shareholders do not have any other investments. The company is looking into investing in a new, bigger car showroom. The financing for the investment will be from internally generated funds.**

Which ONE of the following investment appraisal calculations would be appropriate for Y Ltd to use to assist with the decision-making process?

 A The company's existing Weighted Average Cost of Capital

 B The company's existing Cost of Equity

 C Adjusted Present Value appraisal

 D Capital Asset Pricing Model $k_e = R_f + (R_m - R_f)\beta$

170 **Sonil, is a management accountant for a Z plc a listed international car sales company. It is looking into investing in a new innovative hybrid car. The financing for the investment will be from the issue of a large redeemable debenture which will double the gearing of the company.**

Which ONE of the following investment appraisal calculations would be appropriate for Sonil to use as a basis for decision-making?

 A The company's existing Weighted Average Cost of Capital

 B The company's existing Cost of Equity

 C A risk-adjusted Weighted Average Cost of Capital

 D Capital Asset Pricing Model

171 **Manisha, is a management accountant for a K plc a large manufacturing company. She is undertaking an exercise to calculate the Weighted Average Cost of Capital for the company.**

Which of the following balances should Manisha include in the 'Debt' balance, when calculating WACC? Select all that apply

 A Trade payables

 B Bank loan

 C A rarely used bank overdraft

 D Debenture

172 **M plc is a large listed manufacturing company based in the UK and most of its shareholders are investment funds. The production director is considering the proposal of expanding the company's operations into Asia. The finance director has commented that they will need to reassess the company's required return as their existing calculation is based on the capital asset pricing model (CAPM).**

Which ONE of the following is most likely to be true about the required return?

A   The required return will decrease because of a reduction in unsystematic risk due to diversification.

B   The required return will increase because of a rise in unsystematic risk due to extra risks of the foreign market.

C   The required return will remain unchanged as the level of systematic risk will not change.

D   It is impossible to estimate the impact on the required return without further information regarding the relative betas of the different activities.

173 **Diversification of unsystematic risk within a portfolio of assets held by the company, is ultimately the responsibility of which stakeholder?**

A   The Finance Director

B   The Board of directors

C   A rational investor

D   The Audit committee

174 **The Capital Asset Pricing Model calculates the required rate of return for an individual security.**

Which of the following are variables within the CAPM equation? Select all that apply.

A   The risk free rate of investment

B   The share price

C   The average return on the market

D.   The beta factor

175 **Match the beta value to the relevant required rate of return**

Beta Value	Required rate of return	
A – Beta value less than one	(i)	The shares have more systematic risk than the market average, therefore the investor will require a higher than average return
B – Beta value greater than one	(ii)	The shares have the same systematic risk as the market average, therefore the investor will require an average return
C – Beta value equal to zero	(iii)	The shares have less systematic risk than the market average, therefore the investor will require a lower than average return
D – Beta value equal to one	(iv)	The shares have no systematic risk, therefore the investor will require a risk free rate of return

176

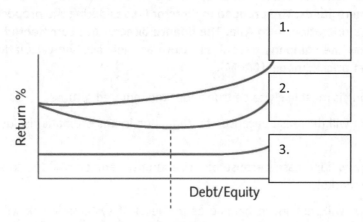

Which ONE of the following CORRECTLY labels the lines on the above graph?

A   1 = Ke, 2 = WACC, 3 = Kd

B   1 = WACC, 2 = Ke, 3 = Kd

C   1 = WACC, 2 = Kd, 3 = Ke

D   1 = Ke, 2 = Kd, 3 = WACC

177 **A company has been trading for 10 months and achieved the following monthly profits:**

(£5,000)   twice

£1,000   three times

£7,000   four times

£12,000   once

Using an Expected Value calculation, which ONE of the following is the average monthly profit?

A   £12,000

B   £7,000

C   £1,000

D.   £3,300

178 Which ONE of the following CORRECTLY labels the lines on the following graph?

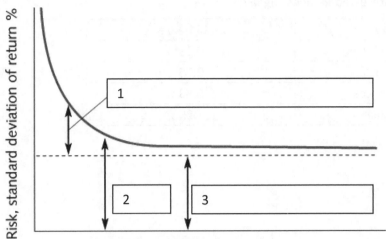

No. of securities in a portfolio

A   1 = Total risk, 2 = Unsystematic risk, 3 = Systematic risk

B   1 = Unsystematic risk, 2 = Systematic risk, 3 = Total risk

C   1 = Unsystematic risk, 2 = Total risk, 3 = Systematic risk

D   1 = Total risk, 2 = Systematic risk, 3 = Unsystematic risk

179 Using your knowledge of the Securities Market Line (SML), recommend which ONE investment would be most suitable for a risk-averse investor who requires an investment only half as risky as the market average?

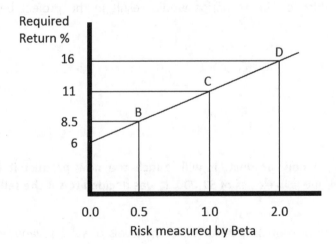

A   Impossible to tell from the information available

B   B

C   C

D   D

180 Using the beta values in the table below, which ONE industry would a risk seeking investor be most interested in investing in?

Industry	Beta Value
Water utility	0.33
Tobacco	0.76
Funeral services	0.83
Advertising	1.25

A   Water

B   Tobacco

C   Funeral services

D   Advertising

181 Winestones, a national bookselling company, is looking at three different potential scenarios for a project under consideration. The project will require an investment of £100,000, will produce net inflows of £55,000 in year 1 and £70,000 in year 2.

The finance manager has produced the following information:

Scenario	Level of risk	Risk-free rate (%)	Risk premium (%)	Risk-adjusted rate (%)
I	Low	9	+3	12
II	Medium	9	+6	15
III	High	9	+10	19

Using the risk-adjusted rate, which of the scenarios would result in the project being accepted? Select ALL that apply

A   Scenario I

B   Scenario II

C   Scenario III

D   Impossible to calculate

182 G plc is considering launching a new product. It will launch the new product if the expected value of the total revenue is in excess of $1,000. It was decided to set the selling price at $10 per unit.

After some investigation, a range of probabilities for different levels of sales revenue has been predicted as summarised in the following table:

Units sold	Revenue	Probability
80	$800	0.15
100	$1,000	0.50
120	$1,200	0.35

Using an expected value calculation, which ONE of the following is the expected revenue for G plc?

A $1,000

B $1,200

C $1,040

D $800

183 D plc is considering whether to make product X or product Y but cannot make both products. The estimated sales demand for each product is uncertain and the following probability distribution of the Net Present Values for each product has been identified.

Product X NPV £	Probability (%)
3,000	10
3,500	20
4,000	40
4,500	20
5,000	10

4000

Product Y NPV £	Probability (%)
2,000	5
3,000	10
4,000	40
5,000	25
6,000	20

44 56

Using expected values, which ONE of the following would you recommend for D plc?

A   Accept Product X

B   Accept Product Y

C   Accept both Product X and Y

D   Accept neither product X nor Y

184 Jamie Jones runs a busy canteen. Based upon previous demand it is expected that, during the 250-day working year, the canteen will require the following daily quantities:

On 25 days of the year   40 salads $0 - 1$

On 50 days of the year   50 salads $0 \cdot 2$

On 100 days of the year   60 salads $0 \cdot 4$

On 75 days on the days   70 salads $0 \cdot 3$

Using the data above, which ONE of the following percentages represents the probability of 70 salads being required?

A   10%

B   20%

C   30%

D   40%

185 Claire, a management accountant at A plc is investigating the company's weighted average cost of capital. She has discovered the capital structure is as follows:

	Cost of Capital %	Book value £m	Market value £m
Bank loans	6	5	5
Debenture loans	10	8	5
Ordinary shares	15	18	30

Using the data above, Which ONE of the following is A plc's weighted average cost of capital?

A   6%

B   10%

C   15%

D   13.25%

$$0.15 \times \frac{36}{40} + 0.06 \times \frac{5}{40} + 0.1 \times \frac{5}{46}$$

$$= 0.1125 + 0.0075 + 0.0125$$

186 J plc is a company involved in housing construction. The planning officer has just been informed of a prime piece of real estate soon to become available. After discussion, the Board of J plc has decided to buy the land for £1 million, as the Finance Director is confident that, even if planning permission is not awarded, the future price of the land will only increase and if the company wishes to sell the land in the future it will be able to make a profit.

Which ONE of the following option types would best describe the Finance Director's argument?

A   An abandonment real option

B   A follow-on real option

C   A timing real option

D   A financial option

187 Cheetah plc is a UK car sales company. The Sales Director is interested in expanding operation into country X. X is a country with a 20% growth rate in GDP and an emerging consumer economy. The Sales Director wishes to enter country X now. However the Managing Director thinks the better choice would to be to delay entry until country X has had a longer period of political stability and the current extensive road building project is completed.

Which ONE of the following would best describe the managing director's thoughts?

A   An abandonment option

B   A follow-on option

C   A 'wait-and-see' option (timing option)

D   A financial option

188 Cleanaway plc, a UK company, manufactures and retails cleaning products. The Marketing Director wishes to sell a new-to-market, innovative mop, which costs £5 to manufacture, for a recommended introductory retail price of £3.99. Her rationale for the loss-leading pricing strategy is that the mop-heads, which need replacing on a regular basis, will be sold for £3, and they cost only 50p to manufacture.

Which ONE of the following would best describes the Marketing Director's thoughts?

A   An abandonment option

B   A follow-on option

C   A 'wait-and-see' option (timing option)

D   A financial option

189 James, a newly-qualified CIMA accountant, is a new member of staff in the finance team at R plc working in the investment project appraisal team. The current investment appraisal technique is familiar to James, as it is fundamentally modelled on a net present value technique. However, the team has just been asked to evaluate the proposal of a significant relocation of the call centre services from the UK to India. The move will be largely finance by a subsidised loan from the Indian government. James has heard his manager say that a NPV calculation will be used as step one to calculate the base case NPV. However, for this appraisal an adjusted present value technique (APV) is more appropriate which also requires a second step as part of the calculation process.

Which ONE of the following best describes the second step of an APV calculation?

A   To calculate a new share price for R plc

B   To calculate the present value of the costs and benefits associated with the finance package

C   To calculate the sunk costs of the relocation

D   To calculate the redundancy cost of the relocation

190 When performing an adjusted present value appraisal, it is necessary to consider separately the financing costs and benefits associated with a new project.

Which of the following costs and benefits would be considered relevant? Select ALL that apply

A   The present value of costs to issue the new financing

B   The present value of new total interest payments to be incurred

C   The present value of the tax shield gained on interest payment

D   The present value of dividends

191 Which of the ONE of the following is the generally accepted primary strategic objective of a commercial company?

A   The maximisation of a company's profit

B   The maximisation of shareholders wealth

C   The pursuit of new opportunities

D   The sustained employment of the work force

192   X plc is a well-known clothing brand has always sourced its clothes from the UK. However it is now considering importing its merchandise from abroad, where the clothing lines can be made at a much lower cost. X plc is also thinking of acquiring a manufacturing subsidiary based in an emerging market.

Based upon the available information, match the stakeholders of X plc with their potentially conflicting goals:

Stakeholder		Goals		
A	Equity investors	(i)	The value for money of products must at least remain, if not improve	B
B	Customers	(ii)	The strategy will need to result in a higher return	A
C	Employees	(iii)	The partnership will end	D
D	UK suppliers	(iv)	Long term security of X plc	C

193   Z plc is an electrical appliances manufacturer. The production director has managed to source a key electrical component for half the price Z plc is currently paying. However, the component, once included in the appliance, will only last half of the time of the current component before it needs to be replaced.

Which of the following conflicts between stakeholder objectives may occur? Select ALL that apply

  ′ A   Long-term customer satisfaction conflicting with a short-term increase in profit

  ° B   Long term shareholder wealth conflicting with a short-term increase in profit

   C   Long term reduction in market share conflicting with a short-term increase in profit

  ⌐ D   Long term brand reputation damage conflicting with a short-term increase in profit

194   Mr Big, the chief executive officer of K plc has just left a meeting with the board of G plc, a market leader in the same industry. The board of G plc have just made an informal bid for K plc offering a premium of 30% above current market value for K's shares. This is a fantastic opportunity for K's shareholders to increase their wealth. However the deal will only apply if Mr Big relinquishes his office. Mr Big has decided to try to dissuade the shareholders of K from accepting the offer.

Which of the following courses of action are appropriate for Mr Big to follow? Select ALL that apply

   A   Mr Big could start a publicity campaign against G plc to try to stop the shareholders of K plc selling their holdings

   B   Mr Big could call an extraordinary general meeting to explain the offer

   C   Mr Big could start buying up shares in K plc

   D   Mr Big could discuss the offer with the non-executive directors of K plc

195 A definition of goal congruence within a control system is 'the state which leads individuals or groups to take actions which are in their [   ] and also in the [   ] of the entity'. (CIMA Official Terminology, 2005)

Which of the following are the words or phrases omitted from the above definition? Select the words or phrases for EACH of the omissions.

A   self-interest

B   area of expertise

C   best interest

D   market

196 Mary is a finance analyst for a small but growing innovative retail company, selling mobile phones via the Internet. The company has only recently listed on the UK stock exchange. At present the company has very few performance indicators. Mary has been tasked with deciding the best measurements to grow the company and ensure survival.

Which THREE of the following indicators would best suit the needs of the company?

A   A year on year increase in sales

B   An increase in market share

C   An increase in the number of hits to their website

D   An increase in cash

E   The number of customers

F   The company's profit

197 D plc is a chain of coffee shops serving fresh ground coffee and pastries. One of the critical success factors (CSFs) is to improve customer satisfaction. Amil, the management accountant of D plc, is looking to measure its performance in a quantifiable way.

Which THREE of the following indicators would best match the CSF identified?

A   An increase in positive customer feedback

B   An increase in market share

C   An increase in the cash flow

D   A decrease in the quarterly number of complaints from customers

E   The number of customers

F   The company's annual profit increasing year on year

198 The public sector is often using the value of money maxim. Within a cancer research charity match the following three elements of the value for money maxim with the appropriate measure.

Element		Measure		
A	Economy	(i)	The number of new treatments available for cancer patients	C
B	Efficiency	(ii)	The cost savings made due to economies of scale	A
C	Effectiveness	(iii)	The number of cancer sufferers helped for every pound spent	B

199 F Ltd is a small privately-owned dentist practice. In recent months, it has experienced severe cash flow problems. However, the owners of the practice feel that the best way forward is to expand the practice into offering more cosmetic dental procedures. The owners are able to finance the practice for a further twelve months with their own funds but after that the practice will have to liquidate if the cosmetic procedures do not generate sufficient income.

Which of the ONE of following investment appraisal techniques would suit the constraints of the dental practice?

A   Net present value appraisal

B   Adjusted present value appraisal

C   A discounted payback calculation

D   Internal rate of return

200 M plc, a large manufacturing company, has just completed a large refurbishment of its head office. Bankole, the management accountant at M plc, has been tasked with investigating why the refurbishment has overspent the budget by 10%. He is considering implementing a post-completion audit.

Which of following are key aims of undertaking a post-completion audit? Select ALL that apply

A   To investigate any variances from budget

B   To provide feedback for future projects

C   To avoid repetition of the same mistakes

D   To save money

201 Which TWO of the following are the most important benefits received from conducting a post-completion audit?

A   A post-completion audit encourages greater realism in future forecasting

B   A post-completion audit highlights the reasons for a successful project

C   A post-completion audit can be used to apportion blame

D   A post-completion audit can be used to cut costs in the current project

202 Which of the following statements is (are) true regarding managerial decisions?

A   The design and use of management control systems affects how an individual makes and implements decisions.

B   Rational managers will always make decisions that are in the best interest of the organisation employing them.

A   Only A is true

B   Only B is true

C   Both A and B are true

D   Neither A nor B is true

203 "Guide Dogs for The Blind" is a charity whose vision is 'for a society in which blind and partially sighted people enjoy the same freedom of movement as everyone else'. It is wholly financed by private donations.

Which ONE of the following performance indicators would be least appropriate to apply to Guide Dogs for the Blind?

    A   Return on capital employed

    B   Number of guide dogs trained

    C   Increase in donations year on year

    D   Reduction in administrative spend per annum

204 S Company has been awarded the contract for the refurbishment of a local hotel. The overall timescale for the project has been agreed at 30 weeks (a very fast completion for this type of project). The timescale is not flexible as the hotel needs to meet this deadline to host a pre-booked wedding. The project has no contingency plan. All other information about the project is vague with the hotel commenting 'we are not the experts; we will let them tell us what we need; after all they should know.'

Which of the following are potential risks to the successful completion of the project? Select ALL that apply

    A   Unrealistic deadlines means overrun is likely

    B   No detailed project plan and specification means misunderstandings between the two parties could occur

    C   The hotel might not pay the bill at the end of the refurbishment

    D   The wedding might cancel

205 W plc is appraising a new capital project using the Adjusted Present Value method. The finance director has collated the following information regarding the project:

Initial cash outflow	£650 million
Annual cash inflow into perpetuity	£90 million
Cost of equity = 15%	
Financing package:	
10 year loan with interest payable at 9%	£400 million
Tax rate = 35%	

Which ONE of the following is the closest Adjusted present value for the project? (to the rounded million)

    A   £280 Million

    B   £57 Million

    C   £31 Million

    D   £2 Million

Section 2

ANSWERS TO OBJECTIVE TEST QUESTIONS

IDENTIFICATION, CLASSIFICATION AND EVALUATION OF RISK

1   B

A full definition of risk should allow for both upside and downside aspects and incorporate the concepts of both probability and impact.

2   D

Risk management is the process of reducing the adverse consequences either by reducing the likelihood of an event or its impact.

3   B

Risk appetite is determined by risk attitude and risk capacity.

4   B

The four strategies in TARA are Transfer; Avoid; Reduce; Accept.

5

Pure risks	Speculative risks
The risk that a fire may destroy company assets	The risk that a foreign exchange rate may change
The risk that a customer goes out of business	The risk relating to the level of future profits
The risk that a virus is introduced to a computer application	The risk that a capital investment may not yield the predicted IRR

Note: Pure risks are only 'downside', whereas speculative risks may be 'upside' or 'downside'.

6 **The six steps in CIMA's risk management cycle are:**

Development of risk response strategy	3
Implement strategy and allocate responsibilities	4
Review and refine process and do it again	6
Identify risk areas	1
Implementation and monitoring of controls	5
Understand and assess scale of risk	2

7

Risk category	Risk
Business risks	Failure of a new product
Economic risks	Inflation rate rises
Environmental risks	Rate of climate change increases
Financial risks	Exchange rate changes

8

Risk category	Risk
Business risks	Raw material prices rise
Economic risks	Disposable income levels fall
Corporate reputation risks	CEO convicted of insider dealing
Political risks	Nationalisation of industry

9

Risk category	Risk
Political risks	Change of Government
Legal risks	Customer sues company for negligence
Regulatory risks	Government increases rate of Corporation Tax
Compliance risks	Company prosecuted for breach of the Data Protection Act

10   A

This is business risk, as it relates to the reputation of product(s), not the Company.

11   B, C, E

12   A, B, C

13   **A, C**

OKJ's risk analysis should focus on key high-impact, high-uncertainty factors in the organisation's environment.

A falls into this category – it is uncertain whether the government will put in place minimum wage legislation but this could have a significant impact on the company's profits. OKJ definitely needs a contingency plan for this.

B is relatively low impact (thanks to OKJ's insurance) and low uncertainty (OKJ seems confident that it will have to pay the fine), so no further analysis is needed.

C is another factor that is high impact (the cost of platinum rising sharply could cause a fall in profits) and high uncertainty (the movement in metal prices is uncertain, as is the likelihood of a recession). Again, OKJ may wish to consider contingency plans here – such as hedging against platinum price movements.

Finally D appears to be highly uncertain (it is not clear how long the CEO will stay with the company), but low impact (the remaining Board of Directors is capable of minimising disruption to the company), so again this is unlikely to be considered a high risk factor.

14

Term	Definition
risk capacity	'the amount of risk that the organisation is able to bear'
risk attitude	'the overall approach to risk'
risk appetite	'the amount of risk that the organisation is willing to accept in the pursuit of value added'

15   **A, C, D**

The number of directors is irrelevant. Although customers may have expectations regarding risk, this is not a direct determinant of risk appetite.

16   **A**

Although both SWOT and PEST(EL) analysis include external or environmental factors, they are used by managers INSIDE the organisation.

17

A   Transfer = 2

B   Accept = 1

C   Reduce = 4

D   Avoid = 3

18   **6 (6MILLION, 6MILLION, $6MILLION, $6MILLION, $6MILLION)**

Once every five years is a probability of 20%. Simply multiply probability and impact to get expected value.

19   **120 (120MILLION, 120MILLION, £120MILLION, £120MILLION, £120MILLION)**

The credit risk exposure is simply the total amount of credit given, not an expected value

20   C

EV = 200 × 0.1 + 250 × 0.4 + 300 × 0.3 + 350 × 0.2 = 280

21   C

22   C, E

23   B

Particularly because it is a small consultancy firm, the death of the CEO would be high impact. However, unless there is a known condition, the probability of sudden death is low.

24   C

High staff turnover is common in the industry so probability is high.

Losing one sales person in a large organisation is unlikely to be anything other than low impact.

25   C

26   B

'Net risk' is calculated by multiplying probability and impact AFTER any action is taken to mitigate the risk.

27   C

28   A, B, C

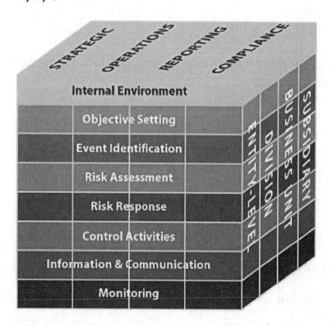

29   A, B, E

COSO considers a WIDE range of risks, and is the responsibility of EVERYONE.

30   All answers are correct

Risk registers record pretty much everything relating to each risk identified

31   A, D, E

The 'missing' elements of the COSO framework are 'Information and communication' and 'monitoring'

32   A

33   B

The Board of Directors are ultimately responsible for a company's system of internal controls.

34   A, C, E

35   B

X has bought a supplier, making it backward vertical integration.

36   A, B, E

C and D are examples of normal business practice.

37   D

MLC have clearly positioned themselves as an ethical company and will therefore attract shareholders who are looking for ethical investments and customers looking for ethically produced goods. If they continue trading with this supplier then their reputation will suffer if the news gets out. By taking strong decisive action and controlling the news story they have demonstrated that they follow their stated ethical principles.

38   ALL OF THEM

39   C

The basic principle here is that of confidentiality. To go outside of the business and professional environment in this manner without first considering the other options presented would not be following recommended process.

A – CIMA's ethics helpline exists to give members advice and is not a breach of confidentiality as it is within the professional arena. B – Reporting the company to the environment agency would comply with relevant legislation, however you would need to sure of your facts before whistle blowing. D – The Audit committee should be all NEDs and therefore a logical place to go, particularly as they are also responsible for the whistle blowing policy.

40   C, D, E

A strong CSR approach may, in fact, increase costs as the organisation has to source its goods more carefully. There is no reason why a strong CSR approach would speed up decision making in the organisation – in fact it is likely to use up management time that could be spent helping to earn the business higher profits. However, CSR often helps to attract both customers and staff, and reduces that chance that governments will be forced to regulate against unethical business behaviour in future.

RESPONSES TO STRATEGIC RISK

41   B, D, F

B – Divisional managers will seek to improve the performance of their divisions but the risk is that the decisions taken may not be in the best interests of the company as a whole.

D – Transfer prices will be needed to correctly account for the expertise and drugs shared between divisions.

F – Performance measures must be fair and motivational to reduce the risk of headhunting.

42   A, D, E

Transfer pricing does not have to be cheap to run, but should ensure that the divisions within Huron work together for the collective benefit of the organisation as a whole.

43   A

$$ROI = \frac{£30,000}{£200,000} = 15\%$$

RI = £30,000 – £24,000 = £6,000.

Since the ROI of the new project exceeds the current after-tax return, it is in the interests of the company to accept it, which the manager of division X will do.

The RI of the project is positive, so will increase the current RI. It will be accepted by the managers.

44   B, E

A – this scheme will be considered unfair and will create a culture of fear, discouraging investment.

B – there is a strong correlation between EVA^{TM} and shareholder value.

C – having two targets could create mixed signals and poor decision making.

D – Managers will still focus on ROI in order to gain the share options, so this will not solve the problem.

E – using NPV will ensure that only projects likely to increase shareholder value are accepted. Using cash flows as a performance metric will motivate managers to achieve the cash flows needed to generate the NPVs calculated.

45   B

The project is acceptable to the company as a whole, because the RI is positive and the ROI exceeds the target return of 10%.

Based on ROI, the manager of division D will be not be willing to undertake the project, as the project will dilute divisional ROI. However, the positive project RI will increase divisional RI.

46   B

The price must be set high enough for TM to cover its costs, but not so high that RM cannot make a profit.

For TM, an item sold externally has VC of 60% × $24.00 = $14.40.

However, of this, $1.50 will not be incurred on an internal transfer so it is not relevant here, giving an incremental cost on internal transfer = $14.40 – $1.50 = $12.90.

We do not know RM's cost structure, so we leave the price at $12.90; this will ensure that RM is not discouraged from taking an internal transfer when it is profitable to do so.

47   A

Selling frames externally, Division A makes positive contribution of £200 – £120 = £80.

If transferred to B, the Company makes overall contribution of £30 (£300 – (£150 + £120)).

Both are worthwhile but selling frames externally should be prioritised.

Note: The current use of a market price approach leads to Div A being indifferent between selling externally and transferring internally. However, Div B will not want to buy frames internally as it generates a divisional loss on bikes made.

48   A, B, E

The Balance Scorecard (BS) includes a range of measures – including longer-term non-financial measures. It also allows each part of the organisation to create its own indicators.

49   A

The variable cost to company is £70 per unit, whereas the cost of buying in is £76. Since Alpha is not fully occupied, by making no Y its profit will decrease (it loses £88 and saves £70). Company profit must decrease because it pays £76 instead of £70.

50   C

Fully autonomous organisations will have control over revenue, cost and investment levels.

51   A

Managers make decisions based on the targets they are set and how they are evaluated. Not all targets will ensure goal congruence with the overall aims of the main organisation.

52   D

You might want to argue that A, B or even C are commercially preferable to D. However, based on the information provided, there is a high likelihood of the Government of E acting in a way that would result in GS paying more tax then it would under option D.

53   A

Out of the 4 Vs, veracity relates to the risk that with so many different sources there is an increased risk of inaccuracies.

54   D

A lack of consultation, concerns over patient care and a lack of a bonus all mean that surgeons are likely to ignore the new targets.

55   C

Ossification refers to an unwillingness to change the performance measurement mix once it is set up – even if the business needs change.

56   A, D, E

A – predictable demand allows a company to anticipate how much to make, thus reducing the need to hold inventories of finished goods.

B – while this can be helpful, it is less important – it is possible to have JiT with a dedicated process that makes just one product.

C – This is irrelevant.

D – this is very important as suppliers may be asked for extra deliveries at short notice to avoid having to hold inventory of raw materials.

E – the smaller the minimum batch size, the easier it is to tailor production to meet individual customer needs.

57

Category	Cost
Prevention costs	Quality circles
Appraisal costs	Inspection of finished goods
Internal failure costs	Re-working rejected output
External failure costs	Customer returns

58

Description	Type of system
These systems allow senior managers to make strategic level decisions	Executive information
N/A	Management information
N/A	Decision support
These systems handle large volumes of operational-level data, and support structured decision making.	Transaction processing
These systems allow any user with basic training to make semi-structured or unstructured decisions.	Expert

59   C, D, E

Managing projects is the role of the Project Managers, while developing new systems will be the job of the project teams.

60   A, C, D

Training and passwords do not mitigate risk in the development process.

61   A, B, D

Pilot changeover cannot be used, as it assumes that any 'lessons learned' in the first changeover can be transferred to all of the other sites. Given each site uses different systems currently it would be difficult to transfer lessons learnt at one site.

62   A, D

Testing reduces the probability of failure, and data backup reduces the impact.

63   A, C, E

64   B, C, E

These are the three major reasons for disclosure of confidential information to third parties.

65   A

Integrity would be compromised as finance professionals should be straightforward and honest.

66   B

Objectivity would be compromised due to the conflict of interest this situation presents.

67   C

CPD is needed to maintain professional competence.

68   D

Divulging the details requested would breach confidentiality.

69

Refuse to remain associated with the conflict	4
Check the facts	1
Escalate externally	3
Escalate internally	2

70   A

John can ultimately benefit financially from his actions so his objectivity may be compromised.

71   C

Gemma is being asked to promote a position or opinion to the point that subsequent objectivity may be compromised.

72   D

Answer D is not a benefit of corporate governance since corporate governance is the set of processes and policies by which the company is directed, administered and controlled and will therefore not prevent fraudulent claims by an external party, i.e. contractors.

Answer A is a benefit since good governance will result in a better image with the providers of finance thus making raising finance easier.

Answer B is also a benefit since good governance should result in sustainable wealth creation.

Answer C is a benefit since customers will prefer to purchase a product or service from a company that has a strong reputation for good governance and hence lower levels of risk.

73   D

Directors, who are placed in control of resources that they do not own and are effectively agents of the shareholders. They should be working in the best interests of the shareholders. However, they may be tempted to act in their own interests, for example by voting themselves huge salaries. The background to the agency problem is the separation of ownership and control – in many large companies the people who own the company (the shareholders) are not the same people as those who control the company (the board of directors).

74   D

External audit is planned by the external auditor. Processing of journals is an operational role and should therefore not be performed by internal audit.

75   B

Chairman and CEO are the two key roles in the organisation and therefore should be held by separate people to dilute power.

76   C, D

77   A, B, C

78   B, C, D

The remuneration committee should consist of independent NED's only and should not consider NED remuneration. This should be decided by the board as a whole and/or shareholders depending on the specific requirements in the company Articles of Association.

79   B

Non-executive directors are required for a balanced board. A chairman needs to be appointed so the roles of chairman and chief executive can be separate.

80   B

Non-executive directors do not take part in the routine executive management of a company, but must participate at board meetings.

81   C

Whilst the best trigger for the awarding of a bonus would be the director achieving a range of individual performance targets, share options would best align remuneration to shareholder interests as both parties would want the company share price to rise to maximise their individual financial return.

INTERNAL CONTROLS TO MANAGE RISK

82

Category	Example
General	Passwords
Application	Check digits
Software	Licenses
Network	Anti-virus software

83

Category	Example
General	Training
Application	Pre-numbered forms
Software	Licenses
Network	Firewalls

84

Security	Integrity
Locked doors	Batch totals
Passwords	Reconciliation
CCTV	Check digits
Fire alarms	Authorisation of data entry

85   **B, D, E**

86   **B, C, D, E**

87   **A**

B will not help improve quality itself and therefore does not link to the CSF identified.

C is not specific – how will the company decide if 'quality' is improved by 50%?

D has no measurable target for the amount of training that will be undertaken.

88   **C**

By definition.

89

Internal Control		Risk
A	Prepare and reconcile budget to actual spend	1
B	Hedging techniques	4
C	Tight stock control systems	3
D	CCTV cameras in store	2

90   **B**

2 is an objective of the purchase cycle. 4 is an objective of the payroll cycle.

91   **D**

1 and 2 are objectives of the purchase cycle.

92   **B**

1 prevents stock-outs/manufacturing delays. 4 prevents unnecessary goods being ordered.

93   **B**

2 prevents stock-outs/manufacturing delays. 3 gives assurance about the quality of goods and reliability of supply.

94 B, C

A – Increased training is more likely to increase the rejection rate.

D – Inspections occur before goods get to finished goods inventory.

E – Employing more quality inspectors is more likely to increase the rejection rate.

95 A, B, D

C – Reducing inventory levels may reduce how much thieves can steal but not the number of thefts.

E – Trying to pass the buck to suppliers is unlikely to affect thefts in X's stores.

96 C

Range checks can help ensure completeness but not security.

97 C

Counterfeiting is a criminal offence and the company may also incur liability for the tort of passing off.

98 A

It would appear that there is no control environment within the company.

99 D

100 B

"Fraud risk is one component of operational risk. Operational risk focuses on the risks associated with errors or events in transaction processing or other business operations. A fraud risk review considers whether these errors or events could be the result of a deliberate act designed to benefit the perpetrator."

(Taken from the CIMA publication "Fraud risk management – A guide to good practice")

101 A, B, C

An effective anti-fraud strategy has four main components – prevention, detection, deterrence and response.

(Taken from the CIMA publication "Fraud risk management – A guide to good practice")

102   A, B, D

CIMA recommends that organisations have:

- a mission statement that refers to quality or, more unusually, to ethics and defines how the organization wants to be regarded externally

- clear policy statements on business ethics and anti-fraud, with explanations about acceptable behaviour in risk prone circumstances

- a route through which suspected fraud can be reported

- a process of reminders about ethical and fraud policies – e.g. annual letter and/or declarations

- an aggressive audit process that concentrates on areas of risk

- management who are seen to be committed through their actions.

(Taken from the CIMA publication "Fraud risk management – A guide to good practice")

103   A

104   A, B, C

105   B, D, E

106   D

This is a classic example of a Ponzi scheme (or a pyramid scheme).

107   C

Management authorisation will increase the chances of fraudulent and inaccurate payments being made to non-existent payables.

108   A, C, D

B will not restore shareholder confidence.

E will please shareholders but do nothing about their confidence that similar frauds will not happen again.

F in unfair to the staff concerned who should not be dismissed without following due process and without good reason.

109   A, B, D

110   A, B, D, E

111

Internal Audit	External Audit
Required by shareholders	Required by statute
Reports to Audit Committee or Directors	Reports to Shareholders and Management
Reports on controls	Reports on financial statements

112

Suggestion	Internal Audit Attribute Standard contravened
Jan, as Head of Internal Audit, should report to the Finance Director	Independence
the first project for the new department should be to audit the Treasury Department, which Jan currently manages	Objectivity
It should not be a problem that Jan has no experience of audit and is only part-qualified.	Professional Care
	None contravened

113 D

Finance staff should not be involved with internal audit work. To ensure errors are identified, someone other than the preparer should review the work.

114 Gap 1 – C (competitive), gap 2 – B (internal), gap 3 – A (process)

Competitive benchmarking is likely to help identify risk areas where the firm is performing much worse (or better) than rivals, but it can be difficult to convince a successful rival to share their secrets. As internal benchmarking focuses on other parts of the same organisation, this type of benchmarking often fails to provide insight into performance compared with rivals but can identify under-performing divisions, for example. Process benchmarking can be difficult as there may be few, if any, non-competing businesses that have the same core processes as our organisation. It is therefore often undertaken for non-core activities.

115 A

Ratio analysis is one type of analytical procedure. An analytical procedure requires evaluation of plausible relationships between financial and non-financial information. Inspection, observation and enquiry are different types of auditing techniques.

116 C

1 is incorrect since internal audit would not retain their independence if they reviewed an area for which they had operational responsibility.

3 is incorrect since internal audit would not retain their independence if they implemented controls; their role is to review the controls once implemented.

2 is correct as ISA 610 allows the auditors to obtain direct assistance from internal auditors under supervision of the audit firm.

117 C, D, E

A – family run companies do not necessarily have weaker controls or higher risks.

B – just because the company is a plc, it does not necessarily follow that it is listed.

F – while one would hope the shareholders would want an internal audit department, this reason is not as important as the other factors highlighted.

118 A, B, C, D

> A – compliance audits check the implementation of rules, regulations and procedures. Checking other stores implementation of the discounting policy would be applicable at B retail.
>
> B – a management audit aims to identify exiting and potential management weaknesses. Auditor may want to judge whether poor management/staff relations for instance may have led to the breaches in procedure.
>
> C – a systems audit would be appropriate: it would examine the objective of discounting stock, how the procedure works and what the current controls are, other ways to manage discounting etc. The entire process of discounting could be reviewed rather than just whether the current policy is being breached elsewhere. It may be the policy is out of date or the EPOS system can easily be overridden.
>
> D – risk based auditing can be applied in this scenario. It may be the breaches occurred in stores that shared staff or where small stores where it may be more difficult to oversee and supervise staff. Audit may therefore choose to focus on such stores as a priority.
>
> E – environmental auditing is concerned with ensuring environmental safeguarding policies and regulations are being met. This is not applicable in this scenario.

119 D

> A systems-based audit is an audit of the internal controls within an organisation. The term can refer to any type of system.

120 A, B, C, D, E

> All of the above may apply. Depending on the audit, certain sections may go into more depth.

MANAGING RISKS ASSOCIATED WITH CASH FLOWS

121 A, B, D, E

> The only factor given that does not directly affect the demand for or supply of a currency is developments in IT.

122 A

> Translation risk relates to the movement in value of assets and liabilities when preparing accounts.

123 C

> The Canadian supplier is unaffected as it invoices in its local currency, the Canadian dollar. It will receive the same number of Canadian $ regardless of any movements of the C$ against the £. Eady plc will have to pay more £ to purchase the C$ payable, so will suffer a loss on the weakening of sterling.

124 B

In a period of rising inflation, the prices of commodities tend to go up, while the prices of shares and bonds often tend to go down. Thus, the commodities position will act as an inflation hedge for the stock and bond portfolio.

125 D

In the context of bonds, interest rate risk is the probability of an increase in interest rates causing a bond's price to decrease.

126 C

Political risk is the possibility of an unexpected politically motivated event in a country affecting the outcome of an investment. Political risk analysis will consider the differences between the home and target country, e.g. the stability of government, corruption by officials, different religious beliefs or ethnic tensions.

127 B

The expected value criterion is independent of risk.

128 B

Gross profit	Overheads	Probability
12	Any	0.1
6	4, 3 or 2	$0.4 \times 0.7 = 0.28$
4	3 or 2	$0.4 \times 0.4 = 0.16$
3	2	$0.1 \times 0.1 = 0.01$

Total = 0.55

129 B, C, D

A and E may have an indirect and relatively minor effect.

130 A, B, D, E

A – Assets in the foreign currency can be offset against the liabilities in the same currency

B – Interest costs will be payable in the foreign currency and can be paid from the income in the same currency – i.e. this allows for netting to occur. Netting is a form of internal hedging mitigating transaction risk.

C – False – Simply having a foreign loan does not reduce the downside risk of interest rates increasing.

D – The stability and state of the local banking system may limit local financing.

E – Raising finance locally may also help to maintain the interest of the local government in the success of the business, and there is less risk that the assets will be confiscated.

EXCHANGE RATE THEORY AND VALUE AT RISK

131 GBP 6,604

Using PPT, the exchange rate in 1 year = 1.5000 × (1.06/1.05) = 1.5143

USD 10,000 then equates to 10,000/1.5143 = GBP 6,604.

132 GBP 1 = EUR 1.2623

Using IRPT, the exchange rate in 1 year = 1.25 − (1.03/1.02) = 1.2623.

133 D

Inflation rates are not relevant to Interest Rate Parity theory (they are relevant to Purchasing Power Parity Theory).

134 7.0%

If the International Fischer effect is true, then the real rate of return in each country should be the same and hence the differences in interest rates can be explained purely due to the differences in inflation.

In Country A the real rate is given by

$1 + r = (1 + m)/(1 = i) = 1.113/1.05 = 1.06$, so r = 6%

Rearranging this equation for Country B,

$1 + i = (1 + m)/(1 + r) = 1.1342/1.06 = 1.07$, so i = 7%

135 B

Applying interest rate parity:

Invest GBP 1,000 at 5.75% for three months (0.0575/4) = GBP 1,014.375

Convert GBP1,000 to EUR at 1.4415 = EUR 1,441.5

Invest that at 4.75% for three months (0.0475/4) = EUR 1,458.62

Implied forward rate is therefore 1,458.62/1,014.375 = 1.4379

136 USD 707 MILLION

The Z value for a one-tail 95% confidence level is 1.645 (from the Normal Distribution tables).

VaR = standard deviation × Z value, so the

VaR = USD 430 million × 1.645 = 707.35 which rounds to 707.

FOREIGN EXCHANGE RATE RISK MANAGEMENT

137 C

Leading with the payment eliminates the foreign currency exposure by removing the liability. Borrowing short-term in Euros to meet the payment obligation in three months' time matches assets and liabilities and provides cover against the exposure. A forward exchange contract is a popular method of hedging against exposure.

138 B

The company will receive Euros through the contracts, so will want a way to sell Euros and receive GBP

A call option gives the holder the right to buy Euros, so is the wrong way round

Forward contracts and MMHs prevent the company from benefiting from any upside potential as they fix the future exchange rate.

139

Internal	External
Leading and lagging	Forward contracts
Matching and netting	Futures
Countertrade	Options

140

Method	Example
Matching	Financing a foreign investment with a foreign currency loan
Netting	Using a foreign currency receipt to offset a foreign currency payment
Pooling	Transferring all bank account balances in one currency into a single account
Countertrade	Exchanging goods or services of similar value

141 A

(1) The investor can buy GBP 500,000 for USD 950,000 compared to USD 975,000 on the spot market.

(2) The investor can sell the GBP 400,000 for SGD 1,160,000 compared to SGD 1,180,000 on the spot market.

The call option should be exercised but the put option should not be exercised.

142 A

First calculate the number of contracts using the STRIKE price so

GBP 5m/1.6 = 3,125,000 then at a contract size of GBP 25,000.

SGB will take an option on 3,125,000/25000 = 125 contracts.

The premium is USD 1,000 per contract so USD 125,000 as a premium must be paid to the exchange when the contract is taken out so this transaction will be done at the current spot of 1.5500.

125,000/1.5500 = GBP 80,645.

143   32,531

X will be looking to buy USD so the starting point is the spot rate of 1.5400

You need to subtract a premium so the forward rate = 1.5400 – 0.0030 = 1.5370

GBP cost = 50,000/1.5370 = 32,531.

144   849,248

The hedge requires X to borrow in GBP, translate to EUR and deposit EUR. The deposit (plus interest) can then be used to pay the supplier.

A payment of EUR 1million in 6 months will require a EUR deposit (earning 1% interest) now of 1,000,000/1.01 = EUR 990,099.

Using a spot rate of 1.195 this requires X to borrow 990,099/1.195 = GBP 828,535. This is borrowed at an interest rate of 2.5%.

Repayment of the loan will cost X 828,535 × 1.025 = GBP 849,248.

145   USD 41,835,000

DWTV will need to BUY GBP to pay their UK supplier and would naturally wish to pay the lowest price per GBP which would be 1.6700, so they exercise the option. (At 1.6700 GBP 25m would cost USD 41,750,000 whereas at 1.6850 it will cost USD 42,125,000)

However they must also have paid the premium of USD 85,000 taking the total cost to 41,750,000 + 85,000 = 41,835,000

INTEREST RATE RISK MANAGEMENT

146

Instrument	Description
Forward Rate Agreement (FRA)	An over the counter instrument, with a fixed rate
Interest Rate Guarantee (IRG)	An over the counter instrument, hedging only downside risk
Future	A traded instrument, with a fixed rate
Option	A traded instrument, hedging only downside risk

147   6.20%

The reference rate of 6.00% is higher than the FRA rate of 5.70% (banks sell high, remember) so the FRA will be settled by a payment to X of 0.30%.

The actual rate paid on the loan is 6.50% (base plus 0.50%), and deducting the FRA receipt of 0.30% gives an effective rate of 6.20%.

148   A

An interest-rate cap will pay its owner the maximum of zero or the market rate minus the cap rate, times the notional principal. An interest rate cap is a bundle of interest rate calls with successive expiry dates, whereas an interest rate floor is a bundle of interest rate puts.

149 D

DD Co pays LIBOR + 1.5% at the moment and the bank has offered a swap at the rate of 5% for LIBOR (i.e. DD Co will pay 5% to the bank in exchange for LIBOR).

Hence the net rate is (LIBOR + 1.5%) + 5% − LIBOR = 6.5%

150 D

There is a bigger difference in the variable rates so to take advantage of this, B will borrow variable and A then has to borrow at a fixed rate.

Use L% to get B on fixed and A on variable. Then 3.5% is the balancing figure to split the saving on an equal basis.

It would work out like:

	Co A	Co B
Paid to bank	(7%)	(L+2%)
A pays B	(L)	L
B pays A	3.5%	(3.5%)
Net effect	(L + 3.5%)	(5.5%)

151 B, C

A   Selling FRAs would be appropriate if Grudem was looking to *deposit* funds.

B   Options to sell STIRs will protect against interest rate rises but allow Grudem to benefit from any falls.

C   Buying an interest rate cap will protect against interest rate rises.

D   Buying bond futures would be appropriate if Grudem was looking to *deposit* funds.

152

Situation	Calculations
Company has a loan and a cap where the strike rate is higher than the market rate	Market rate + premium costs
Company has a deposit and a floor where the strike rate is higher than the market rate	Strike rate − premium costs
Company has a loan and a cap where the strike rate is less than the market rate	Strike rate + premium costs
Company has a deposit and a floor where the strike rate is less than the market rate	Market rate − premium costs

Where the company has a loan we would have to add the premium costs to the loan as in the case of A and C and deduct in the case of a deposit (B and D).

All that then needs to be resolved is whether we exercise the option or allow it to lapse. If we exercise we would use the strike rate if we lapse we would use the market rate.

To determine whether to exercise or lapse we have to consider whether we are looking at a loan or a deposit.

If it is a loan we would want to minimise loan costs so we would pick the lowest rate: in the case of A this would be market rate, which means lapsing the option and using the market rate. Whereas in the case of C the reverse is true we would exercise and use the strike rate.

If it is a deposit we would want to maximise our interest rate returns and therefore if the strike rate is higher than the market as in the case of B, we would exercise the option and use the strike rate (but we deduct the premium costs to get the net benefit).

153

Required position	Combination of options
A 'cap' on the interest rate on a loan	Buy a Call on a FRA
A 'floor' on the interest rate on a deposit	Buy a Put on a FRA
A 'collar' to protect the interest cost of a loan	Buy a Call on a FRA and sell a put on a FRA
A 'collar' to protect the interest on a deposit	Buy a Put on a FRA and sell a call on a FRA

[handwritten notes in left margin: Floor Deposits=puts loans=calls CAP]

Caps place a ceiling on the interest rate costs of a loan, buying the right to buy a FRA will mean that if rates rise the company can buy the FRA and get the counterparty to compensate them, thus reducing the effective loan cost. In a similar way buying a put on a FRA will mean that if rates fall too much they will be able to sell A FRA and benefit from the fall in rates. In the case of the two collars, you will notice that you start the same way as before. In the case of a loan you buy a call paying premium but you simultaneously sell a put thus receiving premium, this reduces the overall premium costs. For a deposit you buy a put in order to protect its value but simultaneously sell a call to reduce premium costs.

154 A

Interest rate options are the right to buy or sell interest rate futures. The option will only be exercised in order to make a profit on the futures which will help to mitigate any losses on a loan due to a rise in interest rates. Interest rate options do not give entitlement to a loan. The loan is taken out independently of the options. An interest rate option does not give the right to an interest rate. It effectively reduces loan costs when interest rates rise adversely by providing a profit on the futures that have been bought or sold.

155 C, D

An interest rate floor would be used for a deposit and not a loan thus the second statement is not true. To achieve this, the company would need to buy a put option on a FRA not a call. Again the last statement will be ruled out as false as floors are used for deposits not for loans. A floor is a means of protecting the interest rate on a variable rate deposit so is particularly useful when interest rates are thought likely to fall. As the premium costs have to be paid this will effectively reduce the interest received on the loan.

156 A, C, D, B

All of these are inputs into the Black Scholes model with the exception of the tax rate.

157 C

Investors 'close out' their positions and therefore either win or lose cash.

158 B

OTC derivative contracts (securities) are customized and have poor liquidity.

The contract is with a specific counterparty and there is default risk since there is no clearing house to guarantee performance.

159 A

The existence of derivatives markets does not affect the level of interest rates. The other statements are true.

160 C, E, F

Options do not provide complete certainty as to the amount paid or received as they may or may not be exercised but they do ensure that the cash flows associated with financing the transaction are known in advance as the premium has to be paid up front regardless of what happens. This is in contrast with futures where there is some variation in cash flows associated with the transaction as variation margin may have to be paid. They are far from being simple, cheap or easy to understand but they are very useful for hedging uncertain transactions as they are a right and not an obligation to do something. In other words they need not be exercised.

MANAGING RISKS ASSOCIATED WITH CAPITAL INVESTMENT DECISIONS

161 C

162 D

163 D

The risk free rate is used, as risk has already been adjusted for by using certainty equivalent cash flows.

164

Projects	Techniques
A – Develop a new range of light weight crossbows. Finance by cutting the forthcoming dividend	Calculate a NPV using the existing company WACC as a discount rate
B – Diversify into making luxury yachts. Finance to be raised to maintain the current gearing ratio	Calculate a NPV using a risk-adjusted WACC
C – Develop a new range of weapons for the police force of Country P. SCW can access a subsidized loan as part of the proposal	Adjusted Present Value
D – Building a new range of fly fishing reels. Finance to be raised via a rights issue.	Calculate a NPV using the existing company WACC as a discount rate

Note:

- The company WACC can only be used if both business risk and gearing remain unchanged by the project.
- A risk adjusted WACC is used when the project has different business risk than the company but the gearing will remain unchanged.
- APV must be used when there is a change in gearing.

165 B

The IRR (C) and the cost of the initial investment (A) are independent of the risk of the project. The higher the risk of the project, then the higher (not lower – D) the required rate of return.

166 A

The use of general purpose equipment makes it easier and less expensive to abandon using the factory if economic circumstances change.

167 252,362

(ACS × 0.95)/0.08 = $3,000,000

ACS = ($3,000,000 × 0.08)/0.95 = $252,362

168 A

Creditors bear the responsibility for bankruptcy in that they will not receive the principal back from their investment. If the project is a great success, creditors' returns will not increase; they will only receive the money loaned plus interest. On the other hand, shareholders could see the value of their shares rise many times over, while the reputation of the managers (and their bonuses) is likely to rapidly increase.

169 C

The project involves a change in the gearing level, so the APV method must be used.

A is wrong as the WACC will change as a result of the project.

B is wrong as the company has debt as well as equity finance.

D is not appropriate as the shareholders are not well-diversified.

170 C

The project involves a change in the gearing level, so the APV method must be used. However, this option is not given, so we must consider which calculations are needed as part of APV. The base case NPV would involve calculating an ungeared cost of equity (not the company's existing Ke) using CAPM, so D is the correct answer.

171 B, D

The WACC calculation should incorporate all long term methods of finance.

172 D

The shareholders are likely to be well-diversified so unaffected by changes in unsystematic risk (A and B). Systematic risk may change as the beta factors in the different markets are unlikely to be the same (C).

173 B

It is a collective responsibility of the board of directors, although it is often delegated to the finance director to deal with on their behalf.

174 A, C, D

175 A (III), B (I), C (IV), D (II)

Beta Value	Required rate of return
Beta value less than one	The shares have less systematic risk than the market average, therefore the investor will require a lower than average return
Beta value greater than one	The shares have more systematic risk than the market average, therefore the investor will require a higher than average return
Beta value equal to zero	The shares have no systematic risk, therefore the investor will require a risk free rate of return
Beta value equal to one	The shares have the same systematic risk as the market average, therefore the investor will require an average return

176 A

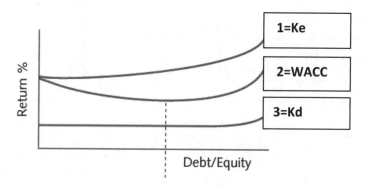

177 D

Outcome (x)	Probability p(x)	x.p(x)
(£5,000)	0.20	(£1,000)
£1,000	0.30	£300
£7,000	0.40	£2,800
£12,000	0.10	£1,200
	E(x)	£3,300

178 C

1 = Unsystematic risk, 2 = Total risk, 3 = Systematic risk

179 B

Having half the risk of the market average implies a beta of 0.5

180 D

Advertising has the highest systematic risk as indicated by having the highest beta.

181 A, B

Scenario I: NPV = −100 + 55/1.12 + 70/1.12^2 = + £1,910

Scenario II: NPV = −100 + 55/1.15 + 70/1.15^2 = + £760

Scenario III: NPV = −100 + 55/1.19 + 70/1.17^2 = − £4.350

182 C

Units sold	Revenue	Probability	Expected Return
80	$800	0.15	$120
100	$1,000	0.50	$500
120	$1,200	0.35	$420
		1.00	$1,040

183 B

Product X NPV £	Probability (%)	Expected value
3,000	10	300
3,500	20	700
4,000	40	1,600
4,500	20	900
5,000	10	500

Total X = 4,000

Product Y NPV £	Probability (%)	Expected value
2,000	5	100
3,000	10	300
4,000	40	1,600
5,000	25	1,250
6,000	20	1,200

Total Y = 4,450

184 C

If 70 salads will be required on 75 days of a 250-day year, the probability that demand:

P(Demand of 70) = 75 days ÷ 250 days

P(Demand of 70) = 0.3

185 D

(5/40 × 6%) + (5/40 × 10%) + (30/40 × 15%) = 13.25%

186 A

187 C

188 B

189 B

190 A, C

Note: interest payemnts are only relevant if, say, a subsidised loan is used, in which case it is the SAVING in interest rates, not the total figure that is relevant.

191 B

192 A (II), B (I), C (IV), D (III)

Stakeholder		Goals	
A	Equity investors	(ii)	The strategy will need to result in a higher return
B	Customers	(i)	The value for money of products must at least remain, if not improve
C	Employees	(iv)	Long term security of X plc
D	UK suppliers	(iii)	The partnership will end

193 A, B, C, D

The reduction in quality is likely to result in a long term fall in reputation, market share, customer satisfaction and shareholder value.

194 B, D

Even though against his own personal interests, Mr Bi g should take steps conistent with maximising shareholder value.

195 A, C

A definition of goal congruence within a control system is 'the state which leads individuals or groups to take actions which are in their self-interest and also in the best interest of the entity' (CIMA Official Terminology, 2005).

196 A, B, D

197 A, B, D

198 A (II), B (III), C (I)

Element		Measure	
A	Economy	(ii)	The cost savings made due to economies of scale
B	Efficiency	(iii)	The number of cancer sufferers helped for every pound spent
C	Effectiveness	(i)	The number of new treatments available for cancer patients

199 C

The emphasis on liquidity makes payback a more suitable technique here

200 A, B, C

201 A, B

202 A

203 A

204 A, B

205 C

Base case NPV = −650 + (90/0.15) = −50

PV of financing side effects = (400 × 0.09 × 0.35) × 6.418 = 80.87

APV = −50 + 80.87 = + 30.87